Indian Mythology

An Enthralling Overview of Myths, Gods, and Goddesses from India

© Copyright 2023 - All rights reserved.

The content contained within this book may not be reproduced, duplicated, or transmitted without direct written permission from the author or the publisher.

Under no circumstances will any blame or legal responsibility be held against the publisher, or author, for any damages, reparation, or monetary loss due to the information contained within this book, either directly or indirectly.

Legal Notice:

This book is copyright protected. It is only for personal use. You cannot amend, distribute, sell, use, quote, or paraphrase any part, or the content within this book, without the consent of the author or publisher.

Disclaimer Notice:

Please note the information contained within this document is for educational and entertainment purposes only. All effort has been executed to present accurate, up-to-date, reliable, and complete information. No warranties of any kind are declared or implied. Readers acknowledge that the author is not engaging in the rendering of legal, financial, medical, or professional advice. The content within this book has been derived from various sources. Please consult a licensed professional before attempting any techniques outlined in this book.

By reading this document, the reader agrees that under no circumstances is the author responsible for any losses, direct or indirect, that are incurred as a result of the use of the information contained within this document, including, but not limited to, errors, omissions, or inaccuracies.

Free limited time bonus

Stop for a moment. We have a free bonus set up for you. The problem is this: we forget 90% of everything that we read after 7 days. Crazy fact, right? Here's the solution: we've created a printable, 1-page pdf summary for this book that you're reading now. All you have to do to get your free pdf summary is to go to the following website:

https://livetolearn.lpages.co/enthrallinghistory/

Once you do, it will be intuitive. Enjoy, and thank you!

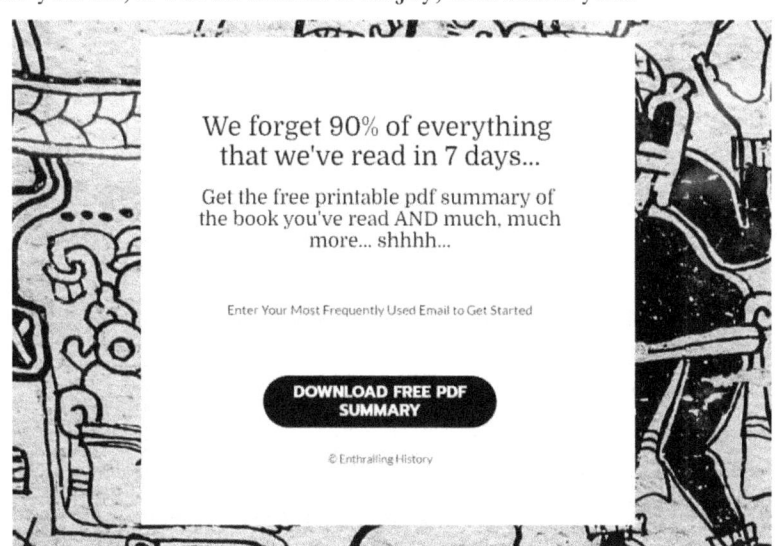

Table of Contents

INTRODUCTION 1
CHAPTER 1: THE HINDU COSMOS 3
CHAPTER 2: VISHNU AND HIS MANY AVATARS 12
CHAPTER 3: SHIVA THE DESTROYER 25
CHAPTER 4: HINDU GODDESSES PART I 36
CHAPTER 5: HINDU GODDESSES PART II 48
CHAPTER 6: KRISHNA THE SUPREME 59
CHAPTER 7: GANESHA, LORD OF LUCK 67
CHAPTER 8: TALES FROM THE *MAHABHARATA* 77
CHAPTER 9: TALES FROM THE *RAMAYANA* 88
CONCLUSION 98
HERE'S ANOTHER BOOK BY ENTHRALLING HISTORY THAT
 YOU MIGHT LIKE 100
FREE LIMITED TIME BONUS 101
BIBLIOGRAPHY 102

Introduction

A perusal of ancient Indian texts reveals intricately woven mythical tales, largely emerging from and influencing religion. Much of Indian mythology centers around the tales of gods and goddesses, the stories of sacred deities, and legends that are interconnected with forces of nature and form significant aspects of the world and life on earth.

Indian mythology largely originates from ancient texts like the Puranas, the Vedas, the *Mahabharata*, and the *Ramayana*. These texts deal with the understanding of life, gods, and creation, acting as a guide into the life of earlier civilizations. In addition to dealing with the spiritual and the religious, these ancient texts also deal with other aspects of living, such as medicine, music, and mantras.

This book is designed to provide a comprehensive understanding of Indian mythology, its various traditions and philosophies, and the ways in which it has created and sustained religious beliefs. In addition to covering the creation of the world, the book also discusses in detail the various deities that play a significant role in Indian mythology and how they contribute to the understanding of the world from a Hindu perspective. It also covers some of the most common tales and legends found in Indian mythology.

The detailed discussion of Indian mythology in this book should help you understand its importance and what beliefs, myths, and legends act as its central basis. Uncover stories that provide insight into everyday life (yes, even today!) and spirituality. We encourage you to form your own conclusions about how these stories might impact people's understanding of the world.

Chapter 1: The Hindu Cosmos

Stories of creation in Indian mythology are categorized under Hindu cosmology and do not originate from any single source. Rather, there are multiple overlapping accounts of how the world came to be. Various texts provide different answers to the question of creation, citing the role of different spiritual forces and deities in creating and maintaining order and balance in the universe.

While the stories of creation in Hindu mythology are interconnected, they are also, in some instances, contradictory. There is no unified basis for Hindu beliefs, and each text may present a wholly different view of the origins of life. Regardless, these beliefs formulate a core aspect of Hinduism, and their contradictory nature may be due to the fact that these mythological accounts were developed at different periods to answer different questions regarding the world's existence.

Creation in the Vedas

The four Vedas, which comprise thousands of texts, each deal with different aspects of life, creation, spirituality, and worship. One of these books is the Rig Veda, the earliest of the ancient Indian texts. Each of the Vedas also includes four key sections, of which the late Vedic Upanishad texts (the most recent addition to the Vedas) deal with philosophical understanding and spirituality.

The Rig Veda

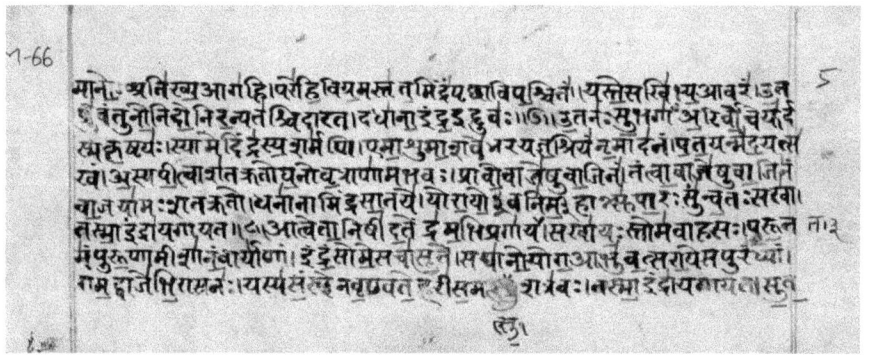

Part of the Rig Veda manuscript.
Ms Sarah Welch, CC BY-SA 4.0 <https://creativecommons.org/licenses/by-sa/4.0>, via Wikimedia Commons; https://commons.wikimedia.org/wiki/File:1500-1200_BCE_Rigveda,_manuscript_page_sample_ii,_Sanskrit,_Devanagari.jpg

The Rig Veda comprises over one thousand hymns in praise of the gods, most prominently Indra. The hymns also deal with the subject of creation. Many of these hymns are still recited during various Hindu festivals. The Rig Veda was originally written in ancient Vedic, which eventually transformed into Sanskrit, and speaks of the life of the Indo-Aryan people in the Vedic age, especially in relation to their questions of philosophy and creation.

Much of the text within the Rig Veda makes use of symbolism and allegory, leaving the text open to interpretation and producing conflicting accounts of the universe's creation.

For example, the Purusha Sukta, a hymn in the Rig Veda, identifies the origins of creation emerging from the destruction of Purusha. Purusha is described as the cosmic being who has always been there and will always be there—an indestructible and eternal universal principle. This being sacrificed itself, and from its body emerged the four kinds of people—the Rajanya, the Brahmin, the Shudra, and the Vaishya.

Another story of creation is the mundane egg or cosmic egg, which forms the physical world around us and was separated into the male-female energy from which life on earth was created. Other creations were also brought into the world, including everything from air and fire to people, the universe, and the gods Agni and Indra.

Upanishads

The Upanishads emerged in the late Vedic period, and they are concerned with understanding the relationship between cosmic powers and humans. The Upanishads talk about the "Self," Atman, which is all that existed in the beginning. While Atman can be understood to mean the soul, it is more aptly translated as the "Self," denoting consciousness, which is the essence of being alive. From the Self emerged the earth and the sky, as well as heaven and hell, which are temporary abodes of rebirth.

The overlapping nature of mythology can be seen in the Upanishads' narration of creation. According to these texts, Purusha existed only as Atman in the beginning and later divided himself into two, male and female, on account of loneliness. Existence then came in pairs. The male embraced the female, and the female, becoming a cow, was embraced by the male as a bull, as well as other animals, such as horses and sheep. Later, the gods and their powers were created, as well as fire and the principles of righteousness.

In essence, the Upanishads show the Self as the beginning of all creation, a non-being from which beings emerged. Since Purusha developed from the Self, he is the beginning of the creation of the world, and by him, life is sustained.

Hiranyagarbha Sukta

Hiranyagarbha Sukta is a hymn in the Rig Veda that talks about the "golden egg" or the cosmic egg, which is thought to be the source of the creation of the universe, existing before creation itself. How this egg came to be the source of creation is a subject of debate. One interpretation of the text suggests that Purusha fertilized an embryo with the natural force, Prakrti, from which the world was created.

Other interpretations view the egg as the source of creation, as the god Brahma emerged from this egg and created the universe and everything in it. Some also suggest that Brahma may have been the egg. Much like the Self, the egg existed before anything else, a non-being from which other beings emerged. While it may be the source of creation according to some texts, the way it created life as we know it is open to interpretation.

Brahmana

The Brahmana texts within the Vedas offer an explanation of the hymns contained in these works and, as such, offer a story on the creation of the world. This story centers around Prajapati, who is the major deity of creation from the Vedic period. While Prajapati has been used to denote various deities in the earlier texts, later Vedic texts refer to him as a single deity and the lord of creation. He is often identified with the Hindu god Brahma.

Prajapati is said to have undergone Tapas, or asceticism, to reproduce with a female partner, sometimes stated to be Vac and other times Ushas. From the first primal water came the golden egg, from which emerged Prajapati. He then created the universe, including everything in it, as well as the Devas (the cosmic deities) and the demigods or Asuras, who, according to some sources, brought about darkness.

The Brahmana speaks of a single line of descent, much like other major religions of the world, like Christianity and Islam, which suggest that the human race is descended from Adam. The Brahmana also describes a great flood that wiped out the human race, leaving only Manu, the last of men. From his sacrifice, the goddess Ida was born, and with her power, the entirety of the current human generation is descended from him.

The Question of Creation: Nasadiya Sukta

Not all texts within the Rig Veda seek to answer the question of the source of creation. Since the texts also deal with philosophical inquiries, the Nasadiya Sukta, known as the Hymn of Creation, poses questions about what led to the creation of the universe rather than seeking to answer them.

This text suggests that any gods credited with the creation of the universe did not exist before it but rather came into existence after the universe was created, leaving the question as to how the world came into being with no gods to create it. The text does not offer any answers or explanations and suggests it may be a truth that can never be known.

Creation in the Puranas

The oldest of the Puranic texts date back to between the 3rd and the 8th century CE. The Puranas deal with the questions of cosmology and establishing the origins of various gods. Many of the books within the Puranic texts are named after gods, discussing where they come from and the role they play in creating and sustaining life. Therefore, the Puranas offer a variety of myths, each offering different explanations of the creation of the world.

Some texts in the Puranas attribute the creation of the world to the god Brahma, tying in the concept of the golden egg, which he may have embodied or from which he may have emerged. Other texts depict a more hierarchical structure of creation emerging from nothing but Brahma, the ultimate universal truth and cause for creation. In other stories, Vishnu, who is part of the Trimurti, is seen as the source of creation. According to these stories, Vishnu created the four-faced god called Brahma. Vishnu's incarnation on earth, Rama, which emerged from a fire sacrifice, is one of the most famous and worshiped incarnations of Vishnu.

Brahma proceeded to create aspects of the universe, including various divine beings and creatures that emerged from parts of his body, such as snakes from his hair and cows from his stomach. The people of the Vedic period came from his body parts and four mouths. Brahma also created a lineage. His wives went on to give birth to other celestial beings and all of creation, including animals and plants.

Brahmanda

The Brahmanda Purana is one of the major Puranic texts. Brahmanda itself refers to the cosmic egg. The text explains the formation of the universe, suggesting that Brahma created and divided the universe into three parts, which were later further broken up into fourteen parts. These realms denote the multi-layered nature of the universe, with some grouped together to create heaven, hell, and earth in a single universe.

The creations that came later, that of living beings and the elements of the earth, were to populate these realms. Some Puranas have suggested the existence of multiple universes, though all of them were created, populated, and destroyed by Brahma. The mythological accounts of the Brahmanda also provide depictions of what the universe looks like, including the radius of the universe and the size and composition of its various elements, such as the stars, the sun, and the moon.

Facets of the Mythology of Creation

The issues of creation within Indian mythology are not limited to simply explaining how the universe came to be. While much of it discusses the role of gods and various deities, mythological texts also explain what these creations were. The ideas of time, matter, and life, which make up the world, are discussed in these texts as well.

Matter

The Vedas, in particular, talk about the elements of matter in the universe. All matter is believed to have three essential qualities or *gunas*:

- Good (*sattva*)
- Darkness or ignorance (*tamas*)
- Passion (*rajas*)

Matter is created when the three qualities are in three possible states. Root matter, Pradhana, occurs in a state of equilibrium when the qualities remain unmixed and unmanifested, that is to say when the three qualities have not interacted with each other to create other matter. Primal matter, or Prakrti, occurs when the *gunas* are mixed but not manifested, creating a state of agitation when interaction has occurred but nothing else has been created. Finally, matter, Mahat-tattva, is created when *gunas* are mixed and manifested into new matter.

Root matter, or Pradhana, cannot act on its own, as the *gunas* within it exist in an unmanifested state. Thus, it lacks consciousness until agitated by a primal desire to create something. Texts do not elaborate on where this desire may emerge from or how the *gunas* interact to supplement creation.

The matter that is finally manifested, Mahat-tattva, ranges from spiritual to individual forms of existence, leading to the creation of intangible elements, such as personality, intelligence, and the mind, and the creation of physical elements, such as space, fire, air, water, and earth, which correspond to the senses and organs created in the human body. Space relates to the experience of sound, fire to the eye, the air to the skin, the tongue to the water, and the nose to the earth.

Time

In Indian mythology, time is cyclic and infinite. Each passing universe will be replaced by other universes in a continuous loop, invariably rendering the question of the source of existence redundant. The creation and the states of matter that make up the universe are guided by time, *kala*, which stretches from the conception of the universe to its destruction, keeping the cycle going for eternity.

The Puranas, the *Mahabharata*, and the *Manusmriti* all speak of an infinite loop of time and are often denoted in terms of the *yuga*, a period of time, and, more noticeably in later texts, as *kalpa*, a day of Brahma. The process of Prakrti, for example, occurs in the span of one Brahma life, a *maha-kalpa*, amounting to over three hundred trillion years. Its matter is destroyed over an equal period of time.

A *kalpa* is over four billion years, the same amount of time it takes for matter to manifest, during which the entire process of creation and destruction takes place, starting over with the next *kalpa*. The partial destruction of matter occurs during the *pralaya*, the night of Brahma, equal in length to a day of Brahma. Each *kalpa* contains one thousand *maha-yugas*, each lasting over four million years and divided into four distinct ages: Satya, Treta, Dvapara, and Kali. Kali is the present time and is seen as a time of wickedness and chaos.

Life

The *jiva-atma* (also called *jiva*), the embodied soul that occupies a temporary home in the human body, is not itself temporary but eternal. It is believed to be neither created nor destroyed. Once manifested, each *jiva* is covered by a *guna* in a distinct manner, which allows various matter to interact with one another. For example, a conscious being, such as a human, interacts with an unconscious matter, such as the mind, which has no physical manifestation.

The material world is *maya*, non-eternal and temporary, existing in states of manifestation and non-manifestation. That is to say that the world simultaneously existed in a physical form for the people who lived on it and as non-physical matter. As such, it is considered a non-reality to the extent that it may be more akin to virtual reality, something that only exists for the people who experience it. *Maya* is denoted by the interaction between *jiva* and temporary objects. A *jiva* begins to identify with its temporary material body through material interactions, entering a state of nescience or ignorance.

Liberation, or *moksha*, for a *jiva* is achieved with self-realization, or *atman-jnana*, leading to the awareness of the true spiritual and eternal identity of the *jiva*. Hindu practice believes the observance of the righteous path, dharma, is essential to achieve *moksha*, which is important to unleash the positive qualities contained in the *jiva*, which are hidden by the *maya*.

The Multiverse

Krishna.
Sujit kumar, CC BY-SA 3.0 <https://creativecommons.org/licenses/by-sa/3.0>, via Wikimedia Commons; https://commons.wikimedia.org/wiki/File:Lord_Krishna.jpg

As the Brahmanda texts indicate, Brahma created multiple universes, each populated with its own creations. The nature of time, as explained within Indian mythology, is such that each of these universes is created and destroyed within a *kalpa*, and many of these universes exist at the same time in fourteen *lokas*, or realms.

The multiverse theory within Hindu mythology speaks of these universes existing at the same time independent of each other. Each universe is ruled by the trinity of the three primary gods: Vishnu, Brahma, and Shiva. Various Puranic and other texts explain the nature of these universes, indicating that each contains the seven elements of earth, fire, water, sky, air, energy, and ego. These universes are also limitless, moving like "atoms" in the grand scheme of creation.

The cyclic nature of time guides the creation, destruction, and re-creation of the universes within the multiverse. Each multiverse dissolves within a *maha-kalpa*, only for the process of creation to begin anew. Another multiverse then emerges, just as large and innumerable as the one before it. Seven higher and seven lower *lokas* exist in each multiverse, although this idea varies depending on the source. Different texts offer different ideas about the multiverse theory.

Chapter 2: Vishnu and His Many Avatars

One of Hinduism's main deities is Vishnu, who is known to be the cosmic guardian and preserver. He is typically depicted as a blue-skinned man with four arms holding items in his hands, usually a conch shell, discus, lotus flower, and mace. The numerous avatars or incarnations that Vishnu has undergone, which are said to be earthly representations of his holy essence, are what distinguish him from other Hindu gods. Hindu mythology holds that Vishnu embraced ten significant avatars, collectively referred to as the Dashavatara, to reestablish harmony and order in the cosmos.

Some of the most fascinating and well-liked myths in Hinduism are those about Vishnu's avatars. Every avatar, from Rama to Krishna, possesses a distinct personality and serves a particular role. For instance, Krishna is viewed as a lovely and mischievous god who epitomizes love and devotion, while Rama is venerated as the ideal monarch and the personification of righteousness.

One interesting thing to note here is that Hinduism is not the only religion in which Vishnu manifests. The legends of Vishnu's avatars have been adopted into a variety of Southeast Asian cultures, including the Javanese and the Balinese. There are several representations of Vishnu's avatars throughout the Angkor Wat temple complex in Cambodia, the biggest religious structure in the world.

We will delve into the intriguing world of Vishnu and his numerous avatars in this chapter. As we explore the tales and legends that surround each avatar, we'll look at their origins, meanings, and symbols. We'll also look at how the idea of an avatar has changed through time, from its roots in ancient Hindu mythology to its contemporary cultural and artistic manifestations.

The Pervader: Lord Vishnu

In Hinduism, Lord Vishnu is worshiped as the defender and preserver of the cosmos. He is known to be one of the main gods. Vishnu is known by various names, one of which is "the Pervader," a reference to his power to express himself in all things and beings in the universe. The three characteristics of existence—*sattva* (goodness), *rajas* (passion), and *tamas* (ignorance)—are said to be embodied in Lord Vishnu. He is thought to permeate every living thing, from the tiniest atom to the huge cosmos. Maintaining the delicate balance between the forces of creation and destruction is crucial to his position as the universe's defender and preserver.

Vishnu belonged to the family of celestial gods known as the Adityas, which sprang from Aditi's womb and were twelve in number (all males). He is thought to have taken many different incarnations on earth, known as his avatars, in order to bring harmony and order to the cosmos.

Avatars of Lord Vishnu

According to Hindu mythology, Vishnu has assumed ten significant avatars collectively referred to as the Dashavatara to reestablish balance in the cosmos. Each avatar corresponds to a certain historical era and reflects a different facet of Vishnu's divinity. The ten avatars are Matsya (fish), Kurma (tortoise), Varaha (boar), Narasimha (half-lion, half-man), Vamana (dwarf), Parashurama (warrior sage), Rama (the hero of the *Ramayana*), Krishna (the hero of the *Mahabharata*), Balarama (Krishna's elder brother), and Kalki (the destroyer of evil). Buddha is occasionally added to the list of Lord Vishnu's avatars in place of Balarama due to the influence of certain sects that regard Buddha as an incarnation of Vishnu. However, Balarama is most commonly believed to be the ninth avatar of Vishnu.

Matsya: The Fish

In Hindu mythology, Matsya, which is Lord Vishnu's original avatar, is a key figure that is believed to have appeared in the *Satya Yuga* (3,747,102 BCE). The Sanskrit term *matsya* means "fish," and the avatar is shown as a huge fish with a human face. The Hindu creation myth, which sees the universe as being destroyed and recreated in a cyclical process, is the source of Matsya's tale.

Matsya is honored in festivals and rituals all over India, where he is revered as a representation of fertility and abundance.

An image of Matsya.
https://commons.wikimedia.org/wiki/File:Matsya_avatar.jpg

The Vedas, which are regarded as timeless truths, were conveyed orally for tens of thousands of years prior to Veda Vyasa's legendary compilation of them in writing. The Vedas were allegedly taken from the universe's creator, Brahma, by the demon Hayagriva. Lord Vishnu took the form of Matsya and dove into the ocean in search of the Vedas. Matsya informed King Manu of an impending flood and gave him the order to construct a boat that could accommodate various varieties of seeds, medicinal herbs, seven saints, the serpent Vasuki, and other animals. And so, Matsya became the protector of life, saving Manu and these other living things.

Water, which stands for both the power of creation and the source of life, is strongly related to Matsya. The fish is regarded as a representation of fertility and abundance. In Hindu art, Matsya is frequently seen holding a conch shell in one hand and a halo of water in the other, signifying his role as the guardian of life. The Matsya avatar has received a lot of praise in contemporary culture, notably in literature, film, and the visual arts.

Kurma: The Tortoise

The second of Lord Vishnu's ten avatars in Hindu mythology is Kurma, also known as Kurmavatara. This avatar also appears in the *Satya Yuga*. The Puranas tell the tale of Kurma, which is regarded as a significant incident in Hindu mythology.

The mythical tale of Samudra Manthan ("the churning of the ocean") serves as the basis for Kurma's origin. According to tradition, the Devas (gods) and the Asuras (demons) collaborated to churn the ocean and acquire the nectar of immortality. The mountain that was being utilized as the churning rod began to sink into the ocean. According to legend, Lord Vishnu transformed into a tortoise and supported the mountain on his back to prevent it from sinking.

An image of Kurma.
https://commons.wikimedia.org/wiki/File:Kurma_Avatar_by_Raja_Ravi_Varma.jpg

The tortoise symbolizes stability, steadfastness, and perseverance. It is viewed as a representation of Lord Vishnu's omnipotence and capacity to support the weight of the entire universe. The use of the tortoise also serves as a metaphor for the earth, which is shown to be perched on the back of a huge tortoise.

The concept of Kurma as an avatar has transformed and been reinterpreted over time in a variety of cultural and creative contexts. Various works of art, such as paintings, sculptures, and folk art, have portrayed the Kurma myth. Throughout India, the avatar can be seen in numerous temples and structures.

Additionally, the narrative of Kurma has been understood from a spiritual perspective in addition to its cultural relevance. The concept of selflessness (in this case, being prepared to carry the weight of the world for the greater good) is represented in the story. It also represents the path taken by the soul on its way to enlightenment.

Varaha: The Boar

In Hindu mythology, Varaha, often known as the Boar, is Lord Vishnu's third form. The word *Varaha* is a proto-Indo-Iranian term for boar (*warajha*). The Varaha avatar, which resembles a boar with a human body, is revered as the guardian of the earth. The concept of this avatar dates to the time of *Satya Yuga*.

One day, the earth was allegedly taken by the demon Hiranyaksha, who concealed it in the depths of the cosmic ocean. Lord Vishnu, assuming the shape of a boar, dove into the ocean to collect the earth. He engaged in a bloody conflict with the demon Hiranyaksha before ultimately defeating him and freeing the earth from his control.

This avatar of Lord Vishnu symbolizes strength and protection. It stands for Lord Vishnu's ability to save the universe from bad influences. The boar represents power, aggression, and tenacity.

Varaha was regarded as a strong and protective sign in antiquity. The earth was thought to be shielded from calamities like floods, earthquakes, and volcanic eruptions by Varaha. Many Hindus still worship Varaha in the modern era. Worshiping the Varaha avatar is thought to aid in overcoming challenges and achieving success in life.

Varaha has appeared in many different forms in contemporary Indian art and culture. The boar-headed Vishnu is shown in paintings, sculptures, and murals. He is shown in some artistic mediums as a ferocious warrior, while in others, he is portrayed as a kind protector. The story behind this avatar serves as a reminder of the need to defend the planet and the need to combat evil powers that pose a threat to the universe.

Narasimha: The Man-Lion

In Hindu mythology, Narasimha, also known as the Man-Lion, is the fourth form of Lord Vishnu's ten avatars and is believed to have appeared in the *Treta Yuga* (2,055,102 BCE). The English name "Narasimha" is formed by combining the Sanskrit words *nara*, meaning "man," and *simha*, meaning "lion." The Narasimha avatar is portrayed as having a human body and a lion's head and is revered as a defender of his followers.

In accordance with the Hindu legend, Hiranyakashipu, the demon king, desired to murder his own son, Prahlada, who was a follower of Lord Vishnu. Hiranyakashipu attained a blessing that made it impossible for him to be slain by anyone or anything at any time of day or night, inside or outside, or by any kind of weapon. At dusk, when it was neither night nor day, Lord Vishnu took the shape of Narasimha, an entity that was neither human nor animal, and killed Hiranyakashipu at the entrance of his palace.

The Narasimha avatar is the representation of protection and justice. It stands for Lord Vishnu's ability to defend his followers from evil powers and promote justice across the cosmos. The human body is a representation of intelligence, wisdom, and compassion, while the lion stands for power, bravery, and fearlessness.

Many Hindus still revere Narasimha in the modern era. Worshiping the Narasimha avatar is thought to foster courage and inner power. For Hindus, the tale of Narasimha serves as a reminder of the value of safeguarding believers and supporting the rule of law.

Vamana: The Dwarf Priest

Lord Vishnu's fifth incarnation in Hindu mythology is Vamana, who is often known as the Dwarf. It is commonly believed that the avatar appeared during the *Treta Yuga*. The Vamana avatar is seen as a representation of humility and selflessness, and it is thought that he took on a human form to impart to humans the value of these attributes.

Bali, the demon king, was said to have acquired invincibility and took over the universe. Vamana requested land he could traverse in three steps when in King Bali's court. Bali granted the request, thinking about what could possibly be covered in three steps. With his first and second steps, Vamana, who had become enormous, covered the earth and the void between it and the heavens. Bali volunteered his head as the third step because Vamana had nowhere else to go for the third step. Vamana put his foot on Bali's head and dispatched him to rule the underworld. In this incarnation, Vamana is referred to as Trivikrama, the "God of the Three Strides."

This avatar represents modesty and selflessness. It serves as a reminder of the value of living simply and giving without expecting anything in return. The Dwarf is a representation of how modest material aspirations are in relation to spiritual wealth's immeasurable riches.

Vamana has been portrayed in many different ways in contemporary Indian art and culture. He is portrayed in diverse stances in sculptures, paintings, and mosaics to represent his many different characteristics. He is shown in certain artistic mediums as a kind and serene divine figure, but in others, he is portrayed as a fearsome warrior.

A sculpture of what is believed to be Vamana.
Sudhamshu Hebbar, CC BY 2.0 <https://creativecommons.org/licenses/by/2.0>, via Wikimedia Commons; https://commons.wikimedia.org/wiki/File:Vamana_Avatar.jpg

Parashurama: Rama with an Ax

One of the ten avatars of Lord Vishnu is Parashurama, also known as Rama with the ax or the "Angry Man." The word "Parashurama" is a combination of the words *parashu*, which means "ax," and Rama, which refers to the protagonist of the epic *Ramayana*. Hindu mythology holds that Lord Vishnu took the form of Parashurama during the *Treta Yuga* when evil and corruption were rampant in the universe.

The tale of Parashurama's birth is told in various Hindu scriptures, but the *Mahabharata* is the most widely read version. This account claims that the sage Jamadagni and his wife Renuka were the parents of Parashurama. Jamadagni, a follower of Lord Shiva, gave Parashurama extensive instruction in martial arts, combat, and devotion. A troop of Kshatriyas (members of the warrior caste), led by King Kartavirya Arjuna, visited Jamadagni's ashram (a place where individuals withdraw spiritually or religiously) one day when Parashurama was gone and requested hospitality.

Jamadagni was a gracious sage, and he welcomed them and provided them with food. The divine cow Kamadhenu, which belonged to Jamadagni, was seen by the Kshatriyas, who desired it and took it by force. King Kartavirya was slain by Parashurama with his ax in a fit of fury. After learning that a Brahmin had killed a warrior, Sage Jamadagni ordered Parashurama on a journey to be purified. When he got back, Parashurama learned that his father had been murdered by Kartavirya's sons. Parashurama slaughtered every warrior from the king's tribe out of rage.

Parashurama's ax, which he handled with tremendous skill and savagery, serves as his emblem. His function as a hunter of evil and defender of good is represented by the ax. A common representation of Parashurama is a powerful man with matted hair, a lengthy beard, and a ferocious look. He is often pictured clutching an ax in one hand.

An image of Parashurama.
https://commons.wikimedia.org/wiki/File:Parashurama_with_axe.jpg

Lord Rama: The Perfect Man

Lord Rama, who is considered one of the most revered deities in Hinduism, is believed to be the seventh incarnation of Lord Vishnu and is also known as Ramachandra. He is frequently referred to as the "Perfect Man" because of his devotion to dharma (righteousness) and his wonderful personality. The avatar is believed to have appeared in the *Treta Yuga*.

Hindu mythology states that Lord Rama was born to King Dasharatha and Queen Kausalya in the northern Indian city of Ayodhya. He was the oldest of four brothers, and his guru (a spiritual teacher), Vishwamitra, instructed him in martial arts and spirituality. Lord Rama is renowned for his unmatched love of his parents, his wife Sita, his brother Lakshmana, and all of creation. In addition, he is well known for his legendary conflict with Ravana, the demon king who kidnapped Sita.

An image of Rama.
https://commons.wikimedia.org/wiki/File:Lord_Rama_with_arrows.jpg

Rama's bow and arrow, which he employed to wipe out evil forces and maintain dharma, serve as his emblem. He is usually seen alongside his wife Sita, his brother Lakshmana, and a fervent follower named Hanuman. Rama has a blue or dark complexion, signifying his ties to Vishnu.

Lord Rama's tale was frequently used as evidence of the significance of upholding one's obligations and adhering to dharma. He was connected to the *bhakti* (devotion or love) movement in medieval times, which emphasized the value of devotion over conventional practices. Lord Rama has come to represent Hindu nationalism in modern times, with his image being exploited to assert Hindu supremacy over other religions and to promote the Hindu identity.

Lord Krishna: The Divine Statesman

One of Hinduism's most beloved gods is Lord Krishna, who is thought to be Lord Vishnu's eighth avatar that appeared in the *Dvapara Yuga* (the third *yuga*). His heavenly nature, intelligence, and role as a leader and warrior are well known. The historical epic *Mahabharata*, as well as the *Bhagavata Purana* and other writings, recount the tale of Lord Krishna.

Hindu mythology states that in the northern Indian city of Mathura, King Vasudeva and Queen Devaki gave birth to Krishna. Father Vasudev escorted Lord Krishna across the turbulent River Yamuna to Gokul in a basket for his protection. Yashoda and Nanda adopted Krishna and brought him up in Gokul. Lord Krishna is renowned for his fondness of cowherd girls (*gopis*), his flute playing, and his fun and mischievous personality.

Lord Krishna's flute and peacock feather serve as symbols. He frequently appears with his beloved Radha, his brother Balarama, and Arjuna, one of his devoted followers. His blue skin suggests that he is connected to Lord Vishnu.

A statue of Krishna at the Sri Mariamman Temple in Singapore.
AngMoKio, CC BY-SA 3.0 <https://creativecommons.org/licenses/by-sa/3.0>, via Wikimedia Commons; https://commons.wikimedia.org/wiki/File:Sri_Mariamman_Temple_Singapore_2_amk.jpg

His teachings in the Bhagavad Gita (a script of seven hundred verses that is a part of the epic *Mahabharata*) were once regarded as a manual for kings and warriors.

The Bhagavad Gita contains an illustration of Lord Krishna's tenacity. The parijata (a kind of lotus flower grown on the heavenly planets) was at the center of a dispute between Krishna and Indra, the king of Heaven. One of Krishna's queens, Satyabhama, asked for the flower, but Indra turned her down. As a result, Krishna and the gods, including the Pandavas (five brothers), engaged in a fierce conflict. In the end, Krishna triumphed, took the parijata flower, and gave it to Satyabhama. He gave Narada Muni the order to tell everyone, including non-devotees, that no demigod could force him to break his word to his queen. Thus, by keeping his word to Satyabhama, Krishna proved his dedication.

Generations of Hindus have been motivated by Krishna's teachings to delve deeper into the nature of reality and the meaning of life. Lord Krishna is still adored and worshiped by Hindus today.

Balarama: Krishna's Elder Brother

Balarama, also known as Baladeva or Balabhadra, is an avatar of Lord Vishnu. He also appeared in the *Dvapara Yuga*. He is frequently shown as a tall, powerful man pulling a plow and is said to be Lord Krishna's older brother.

King Vasudeva and his wife Rohini gave birth to Balarama. He was nurtured in Gokul with his younger brother Krishna under the care of his foster mother, Yashoda. Balarama became renowned for his power and his prowess with a plow, which he used to cultivate the land and defend his people from harm. Balarama wields a plow as his weapon, employing it in various acts. According to the *Bhagavata Purana*, he utilized it to combat demons, create a path for the Yamuna River to reach Gokul, and even shift the entire capital of Hastinapura into the Ganges River.

Lord Vishnu took on the form of Balarama for several reasons. He wanted to get rid of Ravana, the demon king, and help King Yadu run his country. Both goals were accomplished by Lord Vishnu through the avatar of Balarama.

Balarama is seen as a representation of strength and defense. He is frequently linked to the sun, the moon, and the earth, as well as with agriculture. In certain stories, he is also linked to the serpent and is seen as having the ability to tame and control it.

Kalki: The Mighty Warrior

Kalki, also known as Kalkin, is regarded as the final and tenth incarnation of Lord Vishnu. He is thought to be a strong warrior who will make an appearance at the conclusion of the *Kali Yuga*, the current era of darkness and destruction, to bring order back to the universe.

Kalki is depicted as riding a white horse with a sword in his hand. He is portrayed as a savior who will arrive to defeat evil and usher in a brand-new era of stability and harmony.

An image of Kalki on his white horse.
https://commons.wikimedia.org/wiki/File:Kalki_Avatar_by_Ravi_Varma.jpg

Hindu mythology attributes the final victory of good over evil to Kalki, who is frequently portrayed as a figure of hope. He is also viewed as a divine figure who will bring back the universe's natural equilibrium and lead people toward a more peaceful and prosperous future.

Conclusion

The tales of Vishnu's avatars serve as a testament to Indian mythology's enduring beauty. They serve as an insight into the rich and colorful world of gods, goddesses, and heroes and remind us of the virtues of love, fidelity, and righteousness.

Lord Vishnu is worshiped by devotees through a variety of rites and offerings, including chanting his name, reciting his hymns, and giving him flowers and fruits.

Chapter 3: Shiva the Destroyer

Lord Shiva is one of the three principal deities of Hinduism, along with Brahma and Vishnu. He is considered the god of destruction and renewal and is often depicted as a yogi (a practitioner of yoga) who meditates on the peak of Mount Kailash. Many people consider Shiva to be the god of yoga and the arts.

Shiva can be recognized by a number of distinguishing features, including the third eye on his forehead, the snake Vasuki wrapped around his neck, the crescent moon gracing his brow, and the trident that he holds. He is typically venerated as an icon called a lingam. Shiva's teachings emphasize the importance of letting go of attachment and embracing change, both on a personal and universal level. Shiva represents truth, goodness, and beauty and is responsible for the destruction of the ego.

There are many festivals and rituals dedicated to Shiva throughout the year, with the most famous being Maha Shivaratri, or the Great Night of Shiva. This festival is celebrated in late winter and is a time for fasting, meditation, and prayer. To obtain Shiva's blessing and protection, worshipers offer him prayers, flowers, and delicacies.

Image of Shiva.
https://www.pexels.com/photo/photo-of-lord-shiva-statue-in-india-7104962/

Shiva: The Lord of Destruction

The Trimurti is the trinity of the three major gods in Hinduism: Brahma, Vishnu, and Shiva. Brahma is regarded as the creator of the universe, Vishnu as the preserver, and Shiva as the quintessential destroyer. When the end of time comes, Shiva's job is to dissolve all the worlds into nothingness. This idea is in line with current theories of space, which postulate that the expansion of a massive black hole that is consuming material from countless galaxies may cause the end of the physical universe within a few billion years. To Hindus, Shiva may be acting in that capacity as the black hole or as its creator.

It is easy to assume that Shiva's role is limited to destruction, but this is not the case. Shiva has several tasks to accomplish before the world truly comes to an end. His main duty is to eliminate everything to maintain Rta or the order of the universe. Shiva's destruction of things is a positive force that feeds and develops energy for the benefit of the world and its inhabitants. Shiva's devastation aids in nature's evolution, change, and transformation, as well as the smooth passage of objects and occurrences from one phase to the next.

Shiva destroys people's flaws so they can progress spiritually. He destroys their delusions, desires, and ignorance, as well as their evil and negative nature. Shiva also aids in people's personal development by purging their minds of old memories and detaching them from impurities, negative karma, emotions, and any other obstacles that hinder their growth. With his help, it is believed people can move forward and achieve inner enlightenment without any conflict. Shiva can even eliminate death itself. He is the source of life and existence and is thus associated with vitality.

Lord Shiva: The Ascetic Yogi

Lord Shiva is widely revered as an ascetic yogi and is considered the first yogi. It is claimed that Shiva became a traveling ascetic by giving up all worldly pleasures and material goods. He is often depicted as living in remote forests and mountains, meditating for extended periods of time, and subsisting on meager offerings from the natural world. His characteristic attire of a simple loincloth, matted hair, and ash-smeared body demonstrates his ascetic lifestyle.

One of the most significant events in Shiva's life is his meditation on Mount Kailash. Legend has it that Shiva meditated on the mountain for centuries, attaining a state of deep spiritual awareness and enlightenment. During this period, he was known as Adiyogi, or the first yogi, and is said to have imparted the knowledge of yoga to his first disciples, the Saptarishis or the seven sages.

Another important episode in Shiva's life is his encounter with Tripura, three cities that were constructed by Mayasura, a brilliant architect. These cities were prosperous but also impious. Shiva destroyed Tripura with his yogic powers, thereby restoring balance to the universe.

Shiva managed this feat when the gods told him that the Asuras had become evil and stopped worshiping the Vedas. They asked him to stop the Asuras, and Shiva agreed to do so. Shiva asked Vishvakarma, the architect of the gods, to make him a chariot, a bow, and arrows. Vishvakarma obliged, creating a chariot out of pure gold. With Brahma leading it, Shiva rode toward Tripura. At the exact second that the three cities aligned (the cities constantly moved around and only sat in a straight line for a few moments every one thousand years), Shiva launched the Pashupatastra, his most deadly arrow, into the three cities, destroying and burning them instantly.

Another tale suggests that as the cities merged, Lord Shiva only smiled, and his smile set the cities on fire, thus burning them and destroying Tripura.

The Many Forms of Lord Shiva

Lord Shiva is a complex and multifaceted deity with a rich mythology. He is revered by tens of millions of Hindus around the world and is considered an important symbol of the cyclical nature of existence.

Shiva as Mahadeva

Shiva, as Mahadeva, is a prominent deity in Hinduism and holds a significant place in the Shaivite sects of India. Lord Shiva is considered the embodiment of the Supreme Being (Brahma), representing the destructive element of the Trimurti. Mahadeva is associated with destruction, but this is not seen as a negative act but rather as a necessary step in the cycle of creation and renewal.

Some scholars believe that as Mahakala, he destroys and dissolves everything into nothingness, but as Shankara, he reproduces that which has been destroyed and dissolved. Therefore, he is both the creator and the destroyer of the universe.

The lingam, the phallus-shaped symbol of Shiva, represents his reproductive power, which is critical for the cycle of life and creation. As Mahadeva, he is the paramount lord who governs the forces of destruction and creation and the cycles of life and death. He is the ultimate source of all energy and power.

Shiva as Nataraja

Nataraja is the dancing form of Lord Shiva and is one of his most famous and widely recognized depictions. The word "Nataraja" is derived from the Sanskrit words *nata*, which means "dance," and *raja*, which means "king." This representation of Lord Shiva is one of the most well-known Hindu icons, and bronze sculptures of it are still made in some regions of southern India, particularly in the Chidambaram region.

A Chola sculpture of the dancing form of Lord Shiva.
https://en.wikipedia.org/wiki/File:Shiva_as_the_Lord_of_Dance_LACMA_edit.jpg

The Nataraja form of Lord Shiva is considered to be a masterpiece of Chola art. Chola was one of the most powerful Tamil kingdoms during medieval times, hailing from southern India. The Chola sculptures are renowned for their exquisite beauty and intricate detailing.

Shiva as Ardhanarishvara

Ardhanarishvara is a unique and fascinating representation of Lord Shiva and his consort Parvati, the goddess of power and fertility. This deity is often depicted as a figure that combines both masculine and feminine features. The term *Ardhanarishvara* literally means "half-man, half-woman" in Sanskrit.

The iconic image of Ardhanarishvara portrays the god with the right half of his body resembling Shiva, complete with his trademark matted hair, third eye, and trident, while the left half resembles Parvati, with her feminine curves and adorned with jewelry and flowers. This unique fusion symbolizes the inseparable nature of the masculine and feminine energies that exist within the universe, known as Purusha and Prakrti, respectively.

The concept of Ardhanarishvara emphasizes the idea that the divine male and female principles are interconnected and interdependent and that both are necessary for the creation, sustenance, and transformation of the world. Ardhanarishvara is often associated with the idea of balance and harmony and the transcendence of duality, as, in this form, Shiva is half-woman and half-man, being both and neither at the same time. This deity is also sometimes revered as a symbol of divine unity and androgyny, as well as a powerful force for transformation and spiritual growth.

Shiva as Bhairava

Bhairava is a fierce form of Lord Shiva and is associated with death and destruction. He is commonly portrayed with a dog as his mount. Despite his terrifying appearance, Bhairava is renowned as the protector of women and children, and his worship is believed to offer them security and safety. The term *bhairava* is a Sanskrit word meaning "terrible" or "frightful."

According to Hindu mythology, Bhairava was created by Lord Shiva to guard the holy city of Varanasi (also known as Kashi) from negative energies and malevolent spirits. The city is considered to be a sacred site for Hindus, and Bhairava's presence is believed to sanctify and safeguard it. Bhairava is thought to be the protector of the eight cardinal directions, which include north, south, east, west, northeast, northwest, southeast, and southwest. As the guardian of directions, Bhairava is regarded as an omnipresent and all-seeing deity who protects devotees from harm and negative influences.

Despite Bhairava's fearsome reputation, he is revered for his benevolence and compassion. He is often worshiped as a deity who can bestow blessings and boons upon devotees who seek his aid.

Shiva as Pashupati

The term Pashupati is derived from the Sanskrit words *pashu*, meaning "animal," and *pati*, meaning "lord" or "master." Thus, Pashupati is often referred to as the "lord of the animals," reflecting Lord Shiva's close association with the natural world.

Lord Shiva's affiliation with the bull known as Nandi, who is frequently shown as his mount, is one of the most notable ways in which he is connected to animals. The bull symbolizes strength, virility, and fertility and is considered a sacred animal in Hinduism. The bull also represents the steadfast devotion of Lord Shiva's devotees, who are believed to be like Nandi in their loyalty and dedication.

Lord Shiva is also associated with the tiger, which represents power, strength, and fierceness. Tigers are seen as powerful predators in nature and are often used to represent Lord Shiva's fierce and unyielding nature, as well as his role as the protector of the universe.

How Shiva Turned Blue

According to tradition, the Devas and the Asuras, who were cousins, were in constant conflict. However, they eventually agreed to work together to churn the ocean of milk and extract Amrit, the nectar of immortality. They believed that whoever drank it would become immortal and all-powerful. However, Amrit could only be obtained by churning the ocean of milk.

To begin the process, the Devas and the Asuras decided to use Mount Mandara as a churning rod. Lord Vishnu, one of the most important Hindu deities, took the form of a giant tortoise to support the mountain and prevent it from sinking. The serpent king Vasuki, who had a thousand heads, offered himself as the rope to rotate the churning rod. The Devas and the Asuras began vigorously churning the ocean of milk while holding onto Vasuki's head and tail.

As they churned the ocean, a great many things emerged, including precious gems, rare animals, and even the goddess of wealth, Lakshmi. However, the Devas and the Asuras were not satisfied with these treasures; they desired only Amrit. Suddenly, to their horror, the ocean of milk began to churn up a deadly poison called Halahala. The poison was so powerful that it could destroy the entire world. The Devas and Asuras were engulfed in the poisonous cloud, and they began to choke and suffer.

At that moment, Lord Shiva appeared. When he saw the Devas and Asuras in agony, he knew he had to act quickly to save the world. He drank the poison that had emerged from the ocean of milk to prevent it from spreading further. However, the poison was so potent that it began to burn Shiva's insides. He realized that he needed to get rid of the poison before it caused any more damage.

Shiva's consort, Parvati, quickly realized what was happening and clasped her hand around Shiva's neck to prevent the poison from going down his throat. The poison could not pass beyond Parvati's grasp, and as a result, Shiva's throat turned blue, and he earned the name Neelakanta, which means "blue neck" or "blue throat."

Lord Shiva's sacrifice saved the world from destruction, and he gained a permanent reminder of his selfless act in the form of his blue throat. The story of Lord Shiva and the churning of the ocean of milk is an essential part of Hindu mythology.

Marriage of Shiva and Parvati

The marriage of Shiva and Parvati is one of the most popular stories in Hindu mythology. It is said that Parvati, the daughter of the mountain king Himalaya, was smitten by the handsome and powerful Shiva at a very young age. However, Shiva was a hermit who lived in the mountains and was known for his detachment from worldly affairs. He had no interest in marriage or relationships.

Despite Shiva's lack of interest, Parvati was determined to win his heart. She performed intense penance and devotion to Shiva for years, hoping to impress him. She underwent great physical and mental hardships, and her devotion to Shiva was so intense that she even abandoned her luxurious lifestyle and lived like an ascetic.

However, despite all her efforts, Shiva remained unmoved. He saw no need for a companion in his life. Parvati was undeterred and continued to pursue Shiva relentlessly, and her devotion grew stronger with each passing day.

Finally, after years of penance and devotion, Parvati's determination and love for Shiva moved him. He appeared before her and agreed to marry her. Their union is said to have symbolized the union of the male and female principles of creation, which is an essential aspect of Hindu mythology.

Maha Shivratri, one of the most significant holidays in Hinduism, commemorates the union of Shiva and Parvati each year. It is believed that Shiva and Parvati were married on this day, and it is a day of great spiritual significance for devotees of Lord Shiva.

The union of Shiva and Parvati is also important because it resulted in the birth of their two sons, Ganesha and Kartikeya, and their daughter, Ashokasundari. Ganesha is one of the most popular gods in Hinduism and is worshiped as the god of wisdom and success, while Kartikeya is worshiped as the god of war.

Lord Shiva and the Snakes

Snakes have always been considered sacred in Indian culture. Lord Shiva is often depicted with snakes coiled around his neck. This imagery has a significant symbolic meaning and is associated with several stories and legends.

Samudra Manthan, the churning of the ocean, is one of the most well-known legends that explains why Shiva has snakes around his neck. In this tale, the gods and demons were vying for the ocean's nectar of immortality. Several priceless items, including a deadly poison that could wipe out the universe, emerged from the ocean during the churning. Shiva, the universe's guardian, ingested the poison to safeguard the universe.

As the poison was spreading through his body, Vasuki, the king of the snakes, came forward and offered to help him. Vasuki coiled around Shiva's neck and prevented the poison from spreading to his head. This act impressed Shiva, and he blessed and accepted the snake as his adornment.

It is also said that Shiva made ornaments out of the poisonous snake and presented them to his wife Parvati as a gift. The snake on his neck, therefore, represents Shiva's love for his wife.

Vasuki around Shiva's neck.
Foliate08, CC BY-SA 3.0 <https://creativecommons.org/licenses/by-sa/3.0>, via Wikimedia Commons; https://commons.wikimedia.org/wiki/File:Shiva_01.JPG

Covered in Ash

Lord Shiva is often depicted as being covered in ash, which is symbolic of his renunciation of material possessions and his ascetic lifestyle. This depiction of Lord Shiva has its origin in a Hindu story that illustrates the importance of humility and the dangers of pride.

According to tradition, a powerful sage named Parnada was cutting grass when he accidentally cut his finger. Instead of blood, the sap of a tree oozed out. This incident filled Parnada with pride, and he believed that he had become the most pious man in the world, as he did not bleed as people do. Lord Shiva, who witnessed this incident, decided to teach the sage a lesson.

Lord Shiva took the disguise of an old man and asked the sage about the reason for his delight. The sage replied that he had become the most pious man in the world because he no longer bled like a normal human. The old man questioned the sage's joy, saying that it was just sap and nothing to be proud of. He then demonstrated this by slicing his own finger and spilling ash instead of blood.

The sage realized his mistake and begged the god for forgiveness. Lord Shiva forgave the sage and covered him in ash to remind him of the importance of humility and the dangers of pride. The ash also symbolizes the transient nature of material possessions and the ultimate reality of death.

Nataraja and Tandava

Nataraja is one of the most popular representations of Shiva. In this form, Shiva is depicted as a graceful dancer surrounded by a fiery ring that represents the cycle of birth, death, and rebirth. This ring of flames is said to be a metaphor for the eternal energy that permeates the universe.

Nataraja's dance is not just a symbol of beauty and grace but also represents the dynamic interplay between the forces of creation and destruction. Through his dance, he creates new life, sustains it, and ultimately destroys it to make way for a new beginning. In this sense, Nataraja is seen as the embodiment of the eternal process of creation and destruction, which is central to Hindu philosophy.

The tiny demon Apasmara Purusha, which Nataraja is depicted standing upon, represents the negative qualities of ignorance, laziness, and evil thoughts. By dancing on the demon, Nataraja symbolizes his triumph over these negative qualities and his power to overcome them.

The dance of Lord Shiva, known as the Tandava, is said to represent the cosmic dance of creation, preservation, and destruction. The Tandava is a fierce and energetic dance that represents the destruction of the universe. Contrarily, Parvati performs the Lasya, which is a graceful and gentle dance that represents the beauty and joy of creation.

If Lord Shiva were to stop dancing, it is believed the universe would come to an end. Without his constant movement, the world would become stagnant and lifeless, and chaos would reign supreme. Therefore, it is said that Lord Shiva's dance is essential for the survival of the universe and that it will continue for eternity.

Conclusion

Shiva is known for his asceticism, his profound knowledge of yoga and meditation, and his compassion toward his devotees. His stories teach us about the importance of overcoming our ego and desires and embracing our true nature.

Shiva is also revered as the lord of dance and music, and his cultural significance goes beyond his role in Hindu mythology. Numerous pieces of music, literature, and art have been influenced by him, and he has had an impact on many different aspects of Indian culture.

Chapter 4: Hindu Goddesses Part I

Goddesses in Hindu mythology play a vital role in the maintenance of the world and contribute to various aspects of life and living. They are not lesser in power or stature to male deities. Goddesses often hold power over matters of nurturance, procreation, fertility, wealth, and knowledge.

However, not all goddesses mean well. Goddesses can bring happiness and prosperity, but they are also capable of creating great chaos and unrest. Additionally, many of these goddesses appear under various names and titles and as various avatars.

Durga

The goddess Durga.
https://en.wikipedia.org/wiki/File:Durga_Mahisasuramardini.JPG

The goddess Durga goes by many names in the Hindu tradition. The more famous ones include Devi and Shakti, which together mean divine power. Her role in Indian mythology is acting as a commanding force of good, and her existence signifies purity in a world of chaos and destruction. Durga was created as an energy form and unconquerable force of the Supreme Being, Brahma, to supplement the creation and maintenance of the world.

Durga is often referred to as a protective mother. She is the protector of all that is good, pure, and harmonious. The Puranas offer various stories of the creation of Durga, though each of these portrays her as being created as a protector.

One story suggests Durga was created from Shiva's left half of his body. He later created Shiva Loka, at Mount Kailash, with Durga. In another story, the demonic chaos created by Mahishasura, a demon who used his deceit and cunning to defeat the gods, forced Vishnu to take action. He emitted a powerful light from his mouth, whose rays merged and morphed into the goddess Durga, who was able to challenge Mahishasura to a fight. She defeated his vast armies and cut off his head, thus ending his tyranny.

Etymology

The name Durga itself bears witness to the power of the goddess, as it means invincible and indomitable. Deriving from the word *durg*, which means impassable or implies an unconquerable fortress, and the word *gam*, meaning to pass, the name Durga comes to mean one who is beyond defeat, which is the way the goddess is depicted in stories.

The name Durga appears in earlier Indian texts, such as the Vedas, but is not accompanied by her tales of heroism and power that are found in the Puranas. Vedic narrations of the goddess's role portray her as the supreme deity. In other occurrences, Durga is used to refer to different cosmic beings and entities, though they are all powerful and good.

Appearance

Durga is always portrayed with multiple limbs, which signifies her ability to tackle multiple threats at once. She is always prepared to protect the world from evil. Durga's number of arms ranges anywhere from eight to eighteen, and they hold a variety of weapons and divine objects, such as a bow and arrow, javelin, sword, shield, chakra, conch, and a noose. These items help her fight and defeat evil.

She is also portrayed with three eyes. The left eye shows desire by depicting a moon, the right stands for action with the sun, and the middle eye represents fire, which symbolizes knowledge. To show the might of her power, Durga also often appears riding upon a tiger or lion.

The Weapons of Durga

Each of Durga's weapons is meant to aid her against evil, but they also hold symbolic meaning. The conch, for example, represents her connection to the Supreme Being. She holds on to him in the form of sound, as the conch indicates Pranava, or cosmic sound. Durga does not hold the bow and arrow the way one typically would; both are held in one hand, which symbolizes Durga's control over the potential and kinetic aspects of energy.

The chakra or the discus found spinning on her finger symbolizes the world, and the way in which it is held shows her complete control and command over the world. With this control, Durga is able to keep evil at bay and allow the world to walk the path of righteousness. The sword depicts her knowledge, which is sharp and free of doubt, and the lotus shows that her success in defeating evil is certain and also constant, for evil cannot be controlled except by constant struggle.

Durga has also been shown to carry a thunderbolt, which is a sign of her conviction. The trident shows the three qualities of *tamas*, *rajas*, and *sattva* (inactivity, activity, and non-activity, when a state of harmony has been achieved, respectively) to heal and maintain the physical, mental, and spiritual aspects of life.

Avatars of Durga

Durga, like other gods and goddesses in Indian mythology, appears in many different forms or avatars. These relate to the reincarnation process, with Durga appearing in nine different forms. These *Navadurgas*, the collective name for Durga's nine manifestations, include the following:

- Skandamata (stage of motherhood)
- Kusumanda (as the *Mahashakti*)
- Shailaputri (her stage of childhood)
- Kalaratri (stage of destruction)
- Brahmacharini (her period of asceticism)
- Maha Gauri (stage of recovery)
- Katyayani (period as a warrior)
- Chandraghanta (as Shakti)
- Siddhidatri (stage of becoming Mahashakti)

Each of these nine forms is celebrated and worshiped in Hindu festivals, and each represents Durga's powers as a goddess.

Celebration of Durga

Many Hindu festivals celebrate Durga. Durga Puja is a four-day festival that occurs in September or October. The nine-day-long festival of Navratri is celebrated in remembrance of Durga's victory over Mahishasura, and each day celebrates each of her nine incarnations, which are each signified by a specific color.

Durga holds great significance in Hindu mythology and in the hearts of those who practice Hinduism.

Saraswati

Saraswati.
Jean-Pierre Dalbéra, CC BY 2.0 <https://creativecommons.org/licenses/by/2.0>, via Wikimedia Commons; https://commons.wikimedia.org/wiki/File:2_Hindu_deity_Sarasvati_Saraswati_on_ceramic_tile_in_Munnar_Kerala_India_March_2014.jpg

The goddess Saraswati embodies wisdom and is also the goddess of music, speech, and learning. She is often referred to by other names and titles, including Bharati and Shatarupa, which can together mean eloquent existence. Saraswati is also often known as the mother of the Vedas. The Rig Veda contains the first and earliest known mention of the goddess. Later texts credit her with other attributes and achievements as well, such as the invention of Sanskrit. As the goddess of speech, language and learning are her domains, and she is believed to have gifted pen and ink to one of Shiva's children, Ganesha.

While many traditions believe her to be the wife of Brahma, other traditions, such as the Vaishnavas, believe her to have been the wife of Vishnu first. The wisdom shown by Saraswati is the embodiment of Durga's wisdom, and she represents only all that is good. Saraswati often appears in simple white garments, unadorned by jewelry or color, and moves beyond the materialistic world of desire.

The Creation of Saraswati

Saraswati came into being in response to the chaos of the universe. Brahma sought to bring order into the world and was counseled by Durga to bring knowledge into it. From Brahma's mouth emerged Saraswati, riding a swan and dressed all in white, holding books in one hand to represent her wisdom and a veena (a string instrument) in the other to show her mastery of music. Under her guidance, Brahma learned the value of wisdom and began to think, sense, understand, and communicate, which allowed him to create order out of the chaos of the universe.

The melody that Saraswati produced created vital energy, *prana*, throughout the universe, allowing the world to take shape. Since Saraswati was the first being to enter Brahma's world, he became enamored with her and began to desire her. Saraswati rejected his advances, and she did not give in to material desires. She attempted to hide from Brahma as a cow. He followed her as a bull. When she turned into a mare, Brahma morphed into a horse. Despite the continuous chase, Brahma could not catch her in any of her many forms, and thus, she came to be known as Shatarupa, meaning one that can take many forms.

Saraswati and Brahma

Traditions regarding the nature of Saraswati and Brahma's relationship vary. While some portray her as trying to escape Brahma's lust, others show her as the wife of Vishnu. Since Vishnu already had two wives, he gave Saraswati to Brahma. The union of the two is believed to have produced Manu, from whom all of human civilization was born.

Manu survived the famine that killed all of the humans through the nourishment of his mother, allowing him to continue his lineage.

Brahma is believed not to be worshiped as much as the other gods of the Trimurti. A curse is thought to have been placed on him by Saraswati. As the legend goes, Brahma is said to have turned to the gods when Saraswati failed to turn up on time for an important ritual. The delay of this ritual was unacceptable in his eyes. The gods gave him a new wife, Gayatri, to begin the ritual, but when Saraswati saw Brahma with another woman, she cursed him, saying that humanity should never worship him.

Avatars of Saraswati

Saraswati took on many forms. In her original form, she appears with grace and simplicity, dressed in white and riding upon a swan. In addition to the veena and books, she also appears with a rosary and water pot. Her many avatars include the following:

- Medha
- Savitri
- Brahmani
- Gayatri
- Maha Saraswati
- Vāc
- Para Saraswati
- Shatarupa
- Sharada
- Vani
- Aditi
- Bharati

Tales of Saraswati

There are many tales of Saraswati in which she saves the world from destruction. In one such story, Saraswati is able to save Brahma and the world from a demon. The demon intended to seek power so that he could conquer the three worlds—earth, heaven, and hell—and so attempted to appease Brahma to gain power. When the gods turned to Saraswati for help, she outwitted the demon by sitting on his tongue.

When Brahma turned to grant the demon's wish, all he was able to wish for was to never stay awake. The demon found it quite hard to speak with Saraswati sitting on his tongue! Brahma granted his wish, and the demon was put to eternal sleep. His plans to take over the world ended.

Saraswati is also known to have saved the world from annihilation by Shiva. The god found the world in a state of chaos. The people were filled with corruption, and Shiva believed there was nothing left to salvage. As a result, he decided to start over, beginning with the destruction of the existing world so that a new one could be created. He opened his third eye to unleash a fire that would destroy the world and everything living on it.

Saraswati took the form of a river of purity, as fires could only destroy the impure and corrupt. The fire was trapped under the waters and would remain so as long as the world remained peaceful and humans uncorrupted. However, Saraswati warned that should wisdom leave the world, it would be replaced with strife, corruption, and destruction.

Parvati

Parvati and her son, Ganesha.
https://commons.wikimedia.org/wiki/File:Goddess_Parvati_and_her_son_Ganesha.jpg

Parvati is the goddess of love, fertility, and determination. She is also the wife of Shiva and the mother of Kartikeya (also known as Skanda) and Ganesha, the god of war and the remover of obstacles, as well as Ashokasundari, the goddess of harmony. Parvati's name is believed to have been taken from *Parvata*, meaning "mountain." Parvati is also seen as a manifestation of Durga, but this is usually when Parvati is not the consort of Shiva. As the feminine half of Shiva, the two present the duality of existence, the masculine and the feminine.

Parvati is linked to both Durga and Kali, the goddess of time and death. In many depictions, she is seen alongside Shiva, with the two in an intimate embrace. Some depictions portray the two in greater intimacy, with one-half of the body bearing the male traits of Shiva and the other half those of Parvati. This portrayal of the two of them shows the inseparable and dependent nature of the two—neither can exist without the other. When Parvati appears with Shiva, she is seen with two arms, but when she is depicted alone, she can be seen with four arms, carrying various objects in each hand.

The Creation of Parvati

Parvati came into existence to be a wife to Shiva. Shiva withdrew from the world after the death of his first wife. He became lost in mourning and meditation, neglecting to keep an eye on the world, which, in his absence, was overrun by demons from the underworld. The demons created chaos and destruction and sought to take over the world.

In this tale, the gods turned to Shakti (a mother goddess) for help, who proclaimed that only a son of Shiva could defeat the demons and restore order to the universe. As a result, she morphed into Parvati and brought Shiva out of his seclusion to become his wife.

Shiva did not initially take to Parvati, even though she visited him every day in his cave, bringing him fruit. As frustration took over and the world delved deeper into destruction, Parvati asked Kama, the god of desire, for help. He shot an arrow of desire into Shiva, hoping to make him fall for Parvati. However, Shiva did not take kindly to this, and he destroyed Kama with his third eye.

Parvati removed herself from the world, retreating into a forest to sink into meditation and spirituality. She sought no nourishment or shelter. Her devotion finally moved Shiva, who took her as his wife. Together, they had Ganesha and Kartikeya, who defeated the demons of the underworld with the help of Kali.

Parvati and Ganesha

Many texts relate different versions of how Parvati and Shiva's first son, Ganesha, came to be. Some texts, likely written between 1100 and 1400 CE, suggest that Shiva was against having children and told Parvati to create a cloth doll to quench her desire. In this story, the doll becomes enchanted by Parvati's tears, as she longs for a real baby, and these tears transform the doll into her son, Ganesha. Parvati places Ganesha at the mouth of her cave as a guard, instructing him not to let in any strangers.

When Shiva comes to visit Parvati, he does not recognize his son, having never met him before. Ganesha does not recognize his father and refuses him entry. Angered at the commands of a stranger who will not let him see his wife, Shiva cuts off Ganesha's head. Parvati is devastated, so much so that Shiva promises he will make Ganesha whole. He finds the head of an elephant, which he uses to replace Ganesha's head. Thus, Ganesha is reborn and is referred to as the remover of obstacles, owing to the way in which his rebirth occurred.

Lakshmi

Lakshmi.

VedSutra, CC BY-SA 4.0 <https://creativecommons.org/licenses/by-sa/4.0>, via Wikimedia Commons; https://commons.wikimedia.org/wiki/File:Goddess_Lakshmi_is_the_Hindu_Goddess_of_Wealth_and_Prosperity_with_an_Owl_as_her_animal_ride_or_vahana.jpg

Lakshmi is heralded as the goddess of wealth and fortune. As the wife of Vishnu, she showed total devotion to him by taking on various forms to be with him in his many incarnations. For example, in Vishnu's dwarf form, Lakshmi appears from a lotus and is known as Padma or Kamala. In Hindu mythology, the lotus flower represents success and spirituality. The lotus also refers to fertility, representing all of creation in the world, which Vishnu helped create. When Vishnu appeared as the warrior Parashurama, she became his wife as Dharani.

Lakshmi also forms part of the Tridevi, along with Saraswati and Parvati, as the trinity of goddesses in Hindu mythology (the counterpart to the Trimurti). Lakshmi is also referred to in many instances as Lokamata, the mother of the world, and as Lola, which means fickle. The name refers to the ways in which she offers good fortune to people, which can be administered haphazardly.

Appearance

Lakshmi often appears with four arms and hands, much like other gods and goddesses in Hindu mythology. She carries a lotus in two of these hands, which symbolizes purity and success. Each of her four arms is symbolic, as they represent the four goals that every Hindu should follow and strive to achieve. These are dharma, or good conduct; *kama*, desire in life; *artha*, being successful through legitimate means; and *moksha*, which is the liberation from the cycle of life and death.

Unlike the other goddesses of the Tridevi, Lakshmi does not focus on the spiritual. Rather, her role is in the pursuit and achievement of more materialistic aspects. While she plays a maternal role, she is also focused on fulfillment and the granting of desires.

Creation and Rebirth of Lakshmi

The story of Lakshmi's birth and creation varies based on the different texts, most of which date between 300 BCE and 300 CE. In the *Mahabharata*, she comes from the stirring of the milky ocean by the gods.

Indra and Lakshmi were married and had long protected the world from demons. Indra was given sacred flowers by a sage as a gift. Displeased, he threw away the gift. This act of arrogance made the sage angry, who cast a curse on Indra, causing the flowers of the world to wither. This hurt Lakshmi, as one of her many forms included the garland, and she blamed Indra for the disrespect he had caused her. His arrogance made Lakshmi retreat into the milky ocean. Without her, the world was overrun by demons. The gods turned to Vishnu for help, who counseled them to stir the ocean, from which Lakshmi emerged. She rose from the foaming butter, clothed in white and radiating beauty. Vishnu took her under his protection. She resided on his chest, giving him the name Shrinivas, the resting place of Shri, one of the avatars of Lakshmi.

Chapter 5: Hindu Goddesses Part II

Hinduism's practice of goddess worship dates back to the Indus Valley civilization, which arose in the northwest of the Indian subcontinent in approximately 3300 BCE. Figurines of goddesses made of terracotta were discovered during archaeological digs at Indus Valley sites. It is believed they were used in religious rituals.

In the Vedic era, which started around 1500 BCE, the Hindu goddesses were still worshiped. A number of gods and goddesses are honored in hymns found in the Vedas. These hymns portray the goddesses as strong, imaginative, and nurturing deities who bestow favors on their followers.

The worship of goddesses evolved and formalized during the medieval era. Tantra, a spiritual practice that first appeared in India about the 5th century CE, played a part in this too. This is still practiced in Hindu ceremonies today. Harnessing the force of Shakti and achieving spiritual enlightenment are the goals of tantric practices, which include mantras, rituals, and meditations. By the medieval era, the worship of goddesses evolved into a central component of tantric practices, with each goddess representing a distinct facet of Shakti.

Hindus believe in many goddesses, most of whom are linked to motherhood, fertility, and love. Thus, the worship of goddesses is frequently linked to the achievement of worldly goals like money, success, good fortune, and happiness.

Shakti

Hinduism reveres Shakti, also known as Devi or Adi Parashakti, as the most important goddess and the embodiment of feminine strength and creativity. The myths and legends surrounding her have an intricate connection with the history of Hindu goddesses.

The Goddess Shakti.
Soumik Barua, CC BY-SA 4.0 <https://creativecommons.org/licenses/by-sa/4.0>, via Wikimedia Commons; https://commons.wikimedia.org/wiki/File:Adi_Shakti_the_Supreme_Spirit_without_attributes.jpg

Origin and Meaning

The Vedic period is when the idea of Shakti first emerged, personified as the cosmic energy that powers all creation. The goddess is revered as the supreme entity in the Hindu denomination known as Shaktism. Shaktism's origins can be found in the illustrious Indus Valley civilization, whose people placed a strong emphasis on the veneration of the mother goddess. But it wasn't until the medieval era that Shaktism began to emerge as a distinct Hindu tradition.

Many scriptures were written during the medieval period. The Tantras were a collection of ritual manuals that were written from as early as the 7th century CE until the 19th century. During the 18th and 19th centuries, several Shakti-Tantric texts were written with the aim of introducing tantric concepts to the public and increasing their popularity. That's how Shaktism began to grow.

The Bhakti movement, which placed a strong emphasis on devotion to a personal god or goddess, also contributed to the expansion of Shaktism. Devotional poems and hymns to the goddess were written by numerous poets and saints, which contributed to the spread of her admiration.

The Sanskrit word *shak*, which means "to be able" or "power," is where the name "Shakti" originates. Hindus believe that the fundamental, divine energy known as Shakti has the ability to create, maintain, and end the universe. She is linked to fertility, wealth, and the defense of the vulnerable and oppressed.

Attributes and Symbolism

Hindu mythology represents Shakti in several different ways, each with its own characteristics and symbolism. The most well-known manifestations of Shakti are Durga, Kali, Parvati, and Lakshmi.

The yantra and the mandala are two symbolic representations of the concept of Shakti. The mandala is a circular shape that symbolizes the world and how everything is interrelated, whereas the yantra is a geometric design that represents the energy field of Shakti.

Hindu mythology holds that Shakti was created through the fusion of the powers of Brahma, Vishnu, and Shiva.

Kali

The goddess Kali is considered a sacred and fierce goddess in Hinduism. She is frequently depicted as a furious and strong deity who represents both creation and destruction. Typical representations of Kali include her having several arms, wearing a necklace made of severed heads, and standing on a corpse or a demon.

The goddess Kali.
https://commons.wikimedia.org/wiki/File:Kali_by_Raja_Ravi_Varma.jpg

Origin and Meaning

Kali's origins can be found in early Hindu mythology, where it is thought that she is an incarnation of the goddess Durga. In the tale, the demon Mahishasura was so strong that he threatened to rule the universe. The Devas, commanded by Indra, were defeated by Mahishasura in the battle between the gods (Devas) and the demons (Asuras). The Devas combined their divine forces in an effort to find a solution, giving birth to the goddess Durga. Mahishasura was fought by Durga, and Durga prevailed, killing Mahishasura. After the struggle, Durga allegedly transformed into Kali due to her extreme fury.

The Sanskrit word *kala*, which means "time," is the source of Kali's name. The name of this goddess seems fitting because Kali is frequently linked to the universe's constant cycle of creation and destruction. Because of the transient nature of human existence, Kali is frequently portrayed with a necklace of skulls around her neck. Her dark skin serves as a further allegory for the night before morning.

Between about the 6th and 16th centuries CE, India saw the growth of Kali as a deity. Various Hindu literature and religious practices that emphasized the authority and significance of female deities, like Kali, came into being during this time. The *Devi Mahatmya*, which details the struggles of the goddess Durga against many demons and her transformation into Kali, is one important piece of literature from this era.

The story of Kali's conflict with the demon Raktabija is one of the most well-known mythical tales related to her. Raktabija had the ability to turn every drop of his blood that touched the earth into a new demon. Because of this, he was nearly impossible to beat. Raktabija was defeated when Kali drank all of his blood before it could hit the ground.

The concept of Kali has changed over time. In certain cultures, Kali is revered as a protective mother goddess who shields her followers from harm and drives away evil spirits. Other cultures see Kali as a destroyer goddess who brings about the end of the world to make space for a fresh cycle of creation.

With a complex mythology and a variety of manifestations, Kali is still regarded as a significant and widely venerated goddess in Hinduism today. Her roots are difficult to pinpoint in terms of certain historical periods, but her continued significance in Hinduism is a testament to the importance and strength of female deities.

Kamadhenu

Kamadhenu is referred to as the mother of cows or the wish-granting cow. In Hindu mythology, she is worshiped as a celestial entity who can grant the wishes of her followers.

Kamadhenu.

Kamdhenu, CC BY-SA 3.0 <https://creativecommons.org/licenses/by-sa/3.0>, via Wikimedia Commons; https://commons.wikimedia.org/wiki/File:Kamdhenu.jpg

The *Mahabharata*, a Hindu epic, is where Kamadhenu first appears. The gods churned the cosmic ocean while creating Kamadhenu. She was a gift presented to the sage Vasishta and became a representation of prosperity, fertility, and abundance. The goddess Lakshmi, who is connected to wealth and prosperity in Hindu mythology, is frequently associated with Kamadhenu.

Meaning and Depiction

The classic representation of Kamadhenu is a cow with four or more horns and a golden body. She is frequently depicted standing on a lotus or a throne, and she is occasionally joined by a calf or multiple cows. The terms *kama*, which means "desire," and *dhenu*, which means "cow," are the roots of the name "Kamadhenu." This name honors her capacity to grant the wishes of her followers.

Attributes and Symbolism

Her part in the tale of the sage Jamadagni and his son, Parashurama, is one of the most well-known stories connected to Kamadhenu. The milk of Kamadhenu, who belonged to Jamadagni, was thought to have extraordinary healing abilities. When Kamadhenu was taken from Jamadagni's ashram one day, a group of soldiers known as the Kshatriyas drank her milk to treat their wounds. Angered by the robbery, Parashurama launched a campaign against the Kshatriyas, killing them all in the process.

The concept of Kamadhenu in Indian culture has changed over time. According to some beliefs, the goddess Durga is connected with Kamadhenu, who is viewed as a representation of maternity and care. Kamadhenu is revered during festivals and auspicious occasions as a source of material and spiritual wealth.

Kamadhenu continues to be highly regarded and honored in modern Indian culture. In India and other countries in southern Asia, her image can be found in many temples, shrines, and homes. Due to her connection to cows and the significance of cow worship in Hinduism, Kamadhenu has become a political lightning rod in India, with some groups fighting for the protection of cows and others opposing what they regard as the politicization of religious beliefs.

Sita

One of the most cherished goddesses in Hinduism is Sita. She is known as the spouse of Lord Rama, one of Lord Vishnu's incarnations. Her life, her love for her husband, and her devotion to dharma (righteousness) are all reasons why she is one of the most beloved goddesses in Hinduism.

Sita is renowned for her elegance, wisdom, bravery, and constancy. Her tales have been told and commemorated in numerous works of literature and art throughout the ages, and both Hindus and non-Hindus continue to be inspired by her. Millions of Hindus around the world hold Sita in the highest respect and consider her to be one of the most prominent goddesses in Hindu mythology.

Origin and Meaning

Although the precise dates and details are unknown, it is possible to trace the origins of Sita and the *Ramayana* back to ancient Indians. The *Ramayana* is thought to have been composed sometime between 400 and 200 BCE; however, other historians believe it may have been written as recently as the 4th century CE. Sita's story has been altered and reinterpreted by various communities and civilizations throughout India and Southeast Asia for millennia prior to it being written down.

Hindu mythology states that Sita was the daughter of King Janaka of Mithila, a nation that is now Nepal. She was regarded as a wonderful gift from the soil, as Janaka found her in a field that had been plowed. Lord Rama, the prince of Ayodhya, was drawn to Sita when she was a young woman and fell in love with her at first sight. Rama and Sita were wed in a lavish ceremony, but their joy did not last long. Sita made the decision to go into the jungle with Rama when he was banished from his country for fourteen years.

Sita was kidnapped by the demon king Ravana when they were in exile. When he first saw Sita in the forest, Ravana, the demon king with many heads and arms, fell in love with her. Ravana dispatched a golden deer disguised as Rama and Lakshmana to divert their attention away from Sita. He skillfully disguised himself as an elderly beggar and tricked Sita into leaving Lakshmana's protective ring. Taking advantage of the situation, Ravana showed his true self, kidnapped Sita, and took her away in his magical flying chariot to his dominion in Lanka (modern-day Sri Lanka).

Rama engaged in a bloody battle to free Sita from Ravana's grasp. He was assisted by the monkey god Hanuman and an army of monkeys and bears. After vanquishing Ravana and coming back to Ayodhya, Rama had to convince his subjects of Sita's purity, as they questioned her loyalty while she was being held captive.

Sita remained loyal to Rama throughout her struggle, so she made the decision to put herself through a trial by fire (*agni pariksha*) to establish her innocence and defend her honor. She made it through the trial unhurt, and her virtue was confirmed. However, Sita was exiled from Rama's realm after being pressured by his subjects, and she returned to the earth by entering its womb.

Sita's trial by fire.
https://commons.wikimedia.org/wiki/File:Sita%27s_ordeal_by_fire_(cropped).jpg

One of the holiest occasions in Hindu mythology, the marriage of Sita and Lord Rama, is commemorated every year by Hindus all over the world. Tradition has it that the union took place during the *Treta Yuga*, which is thought to have been some 1.2 million years ago.

Another reason Sita is well known is because of her constant love for Lord Rama and her unwavering sense of morality and decency. Sita endured many hardships in her lifetime, including being kidnapped by the demon king Ravana and living in exile with Lord Rama for a number of years, yet she never wavered in her love for him or her dedication to virtue.

Attributes and Symbolism

Sita is respected as a role model for women to follow and is frequently portrayed as a symbol of chastity, virtue, and devotion. She is frequently presented as a kind wife.

As social, cultural, and political settings altered over time, the concept of Sita also changed. In some regions of India, Sita is revered as a fertility and agricultural goddess who bestows favors and wealth upon her believers. The tale of her life is utilized to further moral and ethical principles in other cultures, where she is regarded as a representation of purity. Modern feminist and anti-colonialist movements in India and elsewhere are inspired by Sita, who has emerged as a cultural icon. Some academics contend that Sita's tale might be interpreted as a criticism of the patriarchy and praise women's independence and resiliency in the face of adversity.

Bhumi

Bhumi, sometimes spelled as Bhudevi and Vasundhara, is a Hindu deity linked to fertility and the earth. She is revered as the mother of all creatures and is bestowed with abundant gifts of food, water, and other natural resources. Bhumi is one of the Sapta Matrika, a group of seven mother goddesses revered in Hinduism and frequently grouped together in temples and shrines all over India.

Bhumi is shown as a lovely woman with a contented look. She is frequently depicted sitting or standing on a lotus or tortoise to represent her connection to the earth. She wears green attire, which stands for growth and nature. She wields a mace, a lotus, a plow, and a conch shell in her four arms, each of which stands for a distinct facet of her authority and influence.

Origin and Meaning

Bhumi is frequently seen in Hindu imagery alongside plants that represent development and fertility, such as fruit trees and lotus flowers. Additionally, she is connected to the positive hues of green and yellow. She is sometimes portrayed cradling an infant child, signifying her function as a nurturing and caring mother.

The veneration of Bhumi has changed in style and significance over the years as Hinduism evolved. She is regarded as a local deity in various parts of India. She is revered in other regions as part of a broader pantheon of deities, and elaborate rites and ceremonies have been passed down by practitioners through the ages to honor her.

Attributes and Symbolism

Bhumi has been worshiped since the early Vedic era in ancient India. There are several references to the earth and its significance as a source of life in the Vedas. As a representation of the earth's natural energies and a representation of the divine power that underlies all of creation, Bhumi was probably worshiped in early Vedic rites.

The tale of Bhumi's birth is one of the most well-known tales connected with her. Hindu mythology claims the gods went to Lord Vishnu to request his assistance in defeating the demon Hiranyaksha, who had taken the earth and concealed it in the ocean's depths. In order to fight the demon, Vishnu took the form of a boar and dove into the ocean. He was able to save the earth and put it back in its proper position in the cosmos. During this titanic conflict, Bhumi is supposed to have sprouted from Vishnu's sweat, signifying the close relationship between the earth and the deity Lord Vishnu.

Bhumi's role in the world's creation is the subject of another well-known myth. This story states that the god Brahma, who is credited with creating the universe, asked Bhumi for help in creating the material world. Her influence is evident in the diversity and abundance of the natural world, as well as the fact that she provided the raw materials and natural resources required to form the land, oceans, and skies.

Bhumi's significance increased throughout time as Hinduism developed and broadened to encompass a variety of gods, goddesses, and celestial creatures. Her importance in the Hindu pantheon increased, along with her position as a motherly figure and a source of fertility and abundance.

In order to encourage environmental sustainability and safeguard the earth's natural resources, there has been a resurgence in interest in the worship of Bhumi in recent years.

Conclusion

To sum up, the Hindu pantheon is abundant with a wide range of goddesses that represent various virtues and powers. They continue to have a significant influence on Hindu society today. Each goddess has her own mythology, symbolism, and rituals. From the fierce and guarding Durga to the caring and compassionate Parvati, these goddesses serve as role models for their followers, reminding them of the strength and beauty of the feminine divine.

The worship and adoration of goddesses will surely continue to be an essential component of this age-old and dynamic religion.

Chapter 6: Krishna the Supreme

Krishna, also known as *Kṛṣṇa* in Sanskrit, is one of the most revered and beloved divinities in India. He is worshiped as the eighth incarnation of Vishnu. Over the years, numerous bhakti cults have produced a large amount of religious art, with Krishna serving as their main religious icon.

Krishna's story is primarily drawn from the *Mahabharata*, a Hindu epic, and its 5th-century appendix, the *Harivamsa*, as well as the Puranas. Krishna, the son of Vasudeva and Devaki, was born into the Yadava family.

In order to kill the evil king Kamsa, Krishna and his brother Balarama made their way back to Mathura. The Yadavas, an ancient people who all worshiped Krishna, were then driven to the western shore of Kathiawar, where they constructed Dvaraka, the location of their court. Prince Krishna wed Princess Rukmini, although he also had other spouses.

Krishna's story has had a significant impact on Indian culture, inspiring many forms of art, literature, and music. His teachings on devotion and morality, as expressed in the Bhagavad Gita, a Hindu scripture of the *Mahabharata*, remain influential today.

The Birth Story of Lord Krishna

Lord Vishnu was incarnated as Krishna to protect dharma and spread peace on earth. Because of his dark skin, he was given the name Krishna, which in Sanskrit means "the color of night." Krishna is depicted as a charming boy who plays the flute. He has sparkling eyes, a black or blue complexion, and a celestial shine. The birth of Krishna was a significant event in the history of Hinduism, as the young Krishna was destined to shape the spiritual fate of mankind.

Krishna's birth narrative features his parents, Devaki and Vasudeva, as well as his harsh maternal uncle, King Kamsa. King Kamsa arranged Devaki's marriage with Vasudeva, and during their marriage ceremony, Aakash Vani, a medium for the gods, proclaimed that Kamsa would be killed by Devaki's eighth son. Upon hearing this, Kamsa attempted to kill Devaki with his sword.

Devaki and Vasudeva were devoted and eager to raise children. Unfortunately, Krishna's birth occurred while his mother was in jail. Her evil brother, who was egotistical and power-hungry, had imprisoned her and her husband.

When Krishna was born as Devaki's eighth child, Kamsa was determined to eliminate him. Devaki carried her eighth child in her womb for a year, and on the midnight of Ashtami (the eighth day of the sixth month), she gave birth to Krishna amidst heavy rainfall. Despite being imprisoned, Devaki and Vasudeva prayed for mercy and protection for their child.

In a miraculous turn of events, Vasudeva's chains broke, and the doors to their cell opened on their own. To protect their child from Kasma's wrath, Devaki embraced her child for one last goodbye before entrusting him to Vasudeva, who rushed toward Gokul with Krishna. Along the way, Vasudeva encountered rising waters in the River Yamuna and saw baskets on the riverbank. He placed the youngster in one of the baskets and carried it on his head.

The water level in the river was steadily rising when Vasudeva entered it due to a storm. Then, all of a sudden, the water level began to fall, and a big snake by the name of Shesha came to their aid. At first, Vasudeva was frightened, but he soon realized the snake was there to help him cross the river safely with Krishna. The snake protected the child from the rain and kept his hood spread over Vasudeva until they reached the shore.

Vasudeva and Devaki, before the birth of Krishna, were astonished to see that Yashoda, Nanda's wife (Nanda was a chief and would later become Krishna's foster father), had recently given birth to a baby girl when they arrived at his home. However, their arrival also brought great joy to the household since Vasudeva, Nanda's cousin, had returned after many years. Yashoda's heart broke as soon as she heard Vasudeva tell the couple the tale of his misery. She resolved to save their eighth son at any cost and asked Vasudeva if she could switch her girl with his son so that Kamsa would not become suspicious.

This grand gesture from Yashoda took Vasudeva aback, and he was overcome with tears. He carried the young girl to Mathura in the basket. As soon as he entered the prison, the doors were locked, and the shackles were placed around him once more. The guards were awakened by the girl's crying, and they immediately alerted Kamsa about the eighth birth. As anticipated, Kamsa arrived and took the infant from Devaki, threatening to kill both of them. However, the infant girl abruptly disappeared into the sky and changed into a deity. From above, she warned Kamsa that his destroyer was being raised in Gokul and that his death was imminent.

At Nanda's house, the child was named Krishna and was raised by Yashoda and Nanda as their own. They showered him with love and care, just like they did with Balarama, the elder half-brother of Krishna.

Putana's Unsuccessful Attempt to Murder Baby Krishna

After learning that Devaki's eighth child had survived, Kamsa was distressed and sought a way to kill the baby boy. Putana, a demonic being with a terrifying visage, was instructed by Kamsa to execute all infants in the kingdom under the age of ten days to ensure that Krishna was killed. Because it would boost her reputation and instill fear in others, Putana was eager to accept the assignment. She killed every baby she could find while moving from village to village until she arrived in the community where Krishna lived. There, she discovered information about a unique youngster. She already knew that killing Krishna wouldn't be simple because he wasn't a typical kid.

Putana changed into a lovely lady to trick the villagers and Krishna's foster parents. She asked Yashoda if she could feed the boy, and Yashoda agreed. However, she would have said no if she had known that the stranger had injected lethal snake venom into her breasts. Putana brought Krishna outside and offered him milk that was poisoned. But Putana soon felt as if she was being suffocated by Krishna's strong grip. Krishna held onto Putana even after she changed into a demon to frighten him.

Putana attempted to fly upward to convince the child to let her go, but Krishna drained the life from her and caused her to crash to the ground. The small child was joyfully playing on the demon's body when the shocked townspeople discovered him.

Lord Krishna's Childhood

Krishna's time in Gokul is an essential part of his story. As an infant, Krishna captured the hearts of the *gopis*, the cowherd girls of the village, with his mischievous pranks and miraculous feats, such as killing demons and other things that were beyond the capabilities of ordinary mortals.

Krishna's charm only increased as he grew into a youth. His melodic flute-playing would draw the *gopis*, including the beautiful Radha, the wife of a *gopa* (a cowherd), out of their homes to dance with him in the moonlight. Radha was held dear by Krishna, who remained devoted to him. According to a well-known story, Krishna even saved the villagers from the wrath of Lord Indra, who caused torrential rain in the village. He raised Govardhan Hill with his little finger and used it as an umbrella to shelter the villagers from the deluge.

Krishna's divine power and benevolent nature soon became apparent to all. His uncle Kamsa, who had imprisoned his mother, was still determined to eliminate him. Many assassins were dispatched by Kamsa to kill Krishna, but none were successful. Ultimately, Krishna and his brother Balarama made their way back to Mathura, where they executed Kamsa and established law. Following their triumph, Krishna and the Yadavas (Krishna's clan) relocated to Dvaraka, which is now in Gujarat. He took eight wives there, including Rukmini, a stunning princess from the Vidarbha Kingdom. Ashtabharya is the collective name for his wives.

Kamsa's Failed Attempts to Kill Krishna Led to His Own Demise

Despite Kamsa's repeated attempts to eliminate Krishna, he remained unsuccessful. To get rid of Krishna and Balarama, Kamsa and his servant came up with a fresh strategy. The brothers accepted an invitation to watch a wrestling match in Mathura. They also faced off against two of Kamsa's most powerful wrestlers in the contest, whom they easily defeated.

Kamsa was furious by the defeat and gave the order for his soldiers to kill Krishna and Balarama. However, Krishna stopped them by leaping into the audience and grabbing Kamsa's crown. He then dragged Kamsa by his hair into the wrestling ring. Kamsa challenged Krishna to a wrestling contest in an effort to show off his might, but Kamsa was killed by one strike from Krishna's hand. After Kamsa's death, Krishna set Devaki and Vasudeva, his biological parents, free. This story teaches us that truth and goodness always emerge victorious in the end.

Krishna and Kaliya

Krishna lived a simple life in the village. Each morning, Lord Krishna would take his cows to the river so they could graze. After a while, tragedy stuck. The cows started dying suddenly. And it wasn't just those cows, but everything surrounding the river was poisoned, including the birds that flew over it and the marine life. No one knew what had happened, but Krishna was determined to find out. Krishna discovered that the ten-headed serpent Kaliya lived in the river and was responsible for poisoning the animals that depended upon the river for survival.

Krishna addressed the enormous serpent and pleaded with him to stop tainting the water. Being wicked and obstinate, Kaliya objected. So, Krishna dove into the hazardous water and danced on Kaliya's head.

The villagers gathered around, anxious for the incredible Krishna, but they were stunned at the sight. As time passed, Krishna became heavier and heavier as he danced on top of all ten of Kaliya's heads. Soon, the weight became unbearable for the ten-headed serpent. The dancing actually left an imprint of Krishna's feet on one of Kaliya's heads. Kaliya's wife cried out to Krishna and pleaded for forgiveness. Her cries moved Krishna, and on the condition that Kaliya and his wife cross the river and leave, he would spare Kaliya's life.

Why Is Lord Krishna Called Ranchod?

One of the many names used to refer to Lord Krishna is Ranchod, which has a fascinating origin story. In the time of the *Dvapara Yuga*, Krishna moved to Madhura to protect his Yadava clan from constant attacks by enemies. The Yadava dynasty was assaulted by the unstoppable demon Kalayavana, Jarasandha of Magadha, and other enemies. In order to save the Yadavas, Krishna built the majestic city of Dvaraka in the middle of the ocean and then moved the Yadavas there.

Krishna pretended to flee the battlefield when the men of Kalayavana pursued him. These men were closely followed by the demon. Kalayavana was lured by Krishna into a cave, the latter of whom pretended to flee the battlefield. In the cave, Muchukunda was meditating. Muchukunda, a ruler from the *Treta Yuga* and an ancestor of Lord Rama, had supported Indra in his conflict with the Asuras. Muchukunda sought a long stretch of uninterrupted sleep to revitalize himself after helping Indra win. Additionally, he demanded that anyone who woke him up be burned to ash. Indra granted his wish.

Krishna led Kalayavana into the cave where Muchukunda was sleeping, and Kalayavana accidentally woke him up. Muchukunda's glare burned Kalayavana to ashes. Thus, Lord Krishna earned the name Ranchod, which means "one who flees from the battlefield." This incident showcases Krishna's cleverness and his ability to protect his people from powerful enemies.

Krishna and His Love for Butter

Krishna had an insatiable craving for butter. Gokul, the village where he resided, was well supplied with butter, milk, and curds. Every chance he got, Krishna would take a pot of butter from either his mother or another villager. To keep Krishna from stealing the butter pots, the *gopis* and village mothers began to tie them to the ceiling. They hoped that the small, young Krishna would not be able to reach the pots and that their dairy products would be safe.

However, the cunning Krishna and his companions managed to get the pots by standing on each other's shoulders or rearranging the ceiling tiles. And if that did not give them what they wanted, they would throw stones at the pots and catch the butter with their mouths as it poured down.

When the *gopis* found out, they complained to Krishna's foster mother, Yashoda. She made a commitment to correct him, but instead of doing as he was told, Krishna robbed the *gopis* of their clothing while they were taking a bath in the river. He promised to return their clothes if they vowed to quit whining to his mother.

Unable to correct her unruly son, Yashoda chained Krisna to a large staff. Krishna was able to release himself by moving into the forest with the staff. He became wedged between two trees that were near to one another, but he pulled so hard that he uprooted both, releasing himself in the process. When Yashoda saw her little boy's strength, she realized that he was no ordinary child.

The Great War of Kurukshetra

Arjuna, a Pandava prince, learned to rely on Krishna as a confidant and friend. However, a terrible conflict was brewing between the Pandavas (five legendary brothers) and the Kauravas, the descendants of Kuru, a legendary Indian king. The two sides prepared for war, and Krishna, who wanted to avoid bloodshed, attempted to mediate between the parties. He proposed that the Kauravas grant the Pandavas a small piece of land, but Dhritarashtra (the father of the Kauravas in this story) refused, as he was determined to crush the Pandavas once and for all.

As the situation escalated, Krishna offered to help the Pandavas, but he refused to fight himself, as he believed that violence would only lead to more suffering. Lord Krishna spoke the well-known Bhagavad Gita. He proclaimed, "I am the exclusive creator of this universe, and I can effortlessly destroy my enemies with my 'Sudarshan Chakra' at will. However, I want to educate future generations about the significance of Karma, the act of performing one's duties. One must carry out their duties without being attached to the outcome and avoid being driven by the result. Instead, they should relish the journey of reaching their destination."

Krishna allowed Arjuna to choose between his presence and the loan of his army. Arjuna chose Krishna's wisdom over his troops, recognizing that his advice was worth more than any army. Despite Krishna's best efforts, war was inevitable, and it resulted in the tragic loss of life.

Following the conflict, Krishna went to see Gandhari, Dhritarashtra's aunt. She had lost one hundred of her sons to the battle. She was grieving and angry and cursed Krishna, as she believed he could have prevented the bloodshed. She said that he and his entire dynasty, the Yadavas, would perish within thirty-six years, a curse that came true.

Lord Krishna in Art

Since the 5th century BCE, Hindus have revered Krishna. In Bengal and Udupi, India, in particular, he is regarded as the supreme Hindu deity. Many celebrations are held in his honor, with Krishna Janmashtami being the most well known. On this day, devotees fast for twenty-four hours and present milk-based desserts to the infant Krishna. Wicks are lit at midnight after being steeped in butter as part of the ceremony to celebrate the birth of Krishna.

Krishna is frequently pictured in art as having dark blue or black skin, donning a yellow garment, and sporting a peacock feather in his hair. He frequently appears with cows and plays the flute, a nod to his earlier days as a cowherd. Krishna is also remembered for possessing the Kaumodaki (Lord Vishnu's mace) and the chakra discus of Vajranabha (a Yadava king), both of which were gifts from Agni, the fire god.

The numerous components of Krishna's personality come from several deities. In the 5th century BCE, Vasudeva-Krishna (as in the son of Vasudeva) was worshiped, while Krishna the cowherd was revered as a pastoral deity. In the end, the two came together to form Narayana (an avatar of Vishnu). With Krishna's adolescent liaisons with *gopis* being regarded as indications of a loving interplay between god and the human soul, Krishna's worship also offers a distinctive understanding of the parallels between divine and human love.

Due to the numerous legends surrounding Krishna's existence, there are several paintings and sculptures representing him in various settings. The infant Krishna is frequently portrayed crawling on his hands and knees or dancing merrily while holding a butterball in his lap. Krishna is also shown as a divine lover playing the flute while surrounded by prostrate *gopis*. The image of Krishna being worshiped is one of the most well-known ones.

Lord Krishna: Personal Life

In accordance with popular belief, Sri (Lord) Krishna had sons from each of his eight primary wives. At the time that he killed the demon Narakasura, who was a harsh ruler, it is said that he had 16,100 wives, most of whom came from the Palace of Narakasura. This is interpreted as a manifestation of Sri Krishna's compassion for people who were victimized by outdated social mores and cultural norms.

Rukmini, Satyabhama, Jambavati, Kalindi, Mitravinda, Nagnajiti, Lakshmana, and Bhadra were Sri Krishna's eight primary wives. All ten of Sri Krishna's sons were born to one of these eight queens.

According to an earlier version of the Bhagavata Purana, Sri Krishna is also said to have had a girl named Charumati with Rukmini.

Conclusion

Krishna's life and teachings have been a source of inspiration for people of all ages and backgrounds. His story teaches us about the importance of love, friendship, devotion, and sacrifice. Krishna's message is universal and relevant today as we strive to find meaning and purpose in our lives.

Krishna's life was full of challenges, but he faced them with grace and wisdom. His teachings continue to provide guidance to people seeking to live a life of purpose, meaning, and service. Through his life and teachings, Krishna has left an indelible mark on Hinduism and the world, and his legacy will continue to inspire generations to come.

Chapter 7: Ganesha, Lord of Luck

Ganesha, also known as Ganesh, is referred to as the Remover of Obstacles. The story of his birth, of coming to life from Parvati's tears and being beheaded by his father, who replaced his head with that of an elephant, also gave him the title of the Lord of Luck and the Lord of New Beginnings. He is a revered and celebrated deity, and as the Lord of New Beginnings, he is often invoked at the beginning of religious ceremonies.

While some texts relate his origins to Shiva and Parvati, some traditions, in particular, the Ganapatya, believe Ganesha to be the Supreme Being. Aside from his most notable attribute, the elephant head, Ganesha is also known as the patron of knowledge, the arts, sciences, and wisdom. His avatar names include Ganapati, Vinayaka, and Pillaiyar.

Appearance

Ganesha

Pradeep Kumar Sharma, CC BY-SA 4.0 <https://creativecommons.org/licenses/by-sa/4.0>, via Wikimedia Commons. Image has been cropped. https://commons.wikimedia.org/wiki/File:Lord-ganesha-22.jpg

The Ganesha Purana, written somewhere between 1100 and 1400 CE, offers the greatest insight into Ganesha. He is depicted with an elephant head in texts. Although the story of Shiva replacing his head with that of an elephant is the most popular, other explanations exist.

Some texts suggest that Ganesha was simply born with an elephant head. Another suggests that Ganesha was born by Shiva's laughter. His form made Shiva jealous, as he considered him too physically alluring. In response, Shiva gave his son the head of an elephant and a protruding belly. Certain texts also state that Ganesha had five elephant heads instead of one head.

Ganesha has been regularly depicted with a single tusk, and mythological texts state that the other tusk was broken. As such, he is also known as Ekadanta, one-tusked, although this name is also attributed to his second incarnation. In his second reincarnation, Ganesha emerges as Ekadanta and travels upon a mouse to defeat the demon Madasur. In some imagery, Ganesha holds his broken tusk in one hand.

Ganesha's round belly became a rather distinctive attribute and can be seen in pictorial depictions and statues that emerged between the 4th and 6th centuries CE. The feature is important enough to have two of Ganesha's incarnations named after it: Lambodara and Mahodara, meaning "hanging belly" and "great belly," respectively. Ganesha's belly is also symbolic, as it is believed to hold all of the universes, the past, present, and future.

Many gods and goddesses in Indian mythology are portrayed with more than two arms, and Ganesha is no different, although the number of his arms varies based on texts, with his more famous depictions having up to sixteen arms. The most common depictions, particularly in the Puranas, have four arms, although up to twenty arms can be seen in certain depictions between the 9th and 10th centuries. Ganesha also often appears with a serpent, sometimes wrapped around his neck, ankles, or stomach, or as a sacred thread held in one hand. Sometimes, Ganesha sits on a throne.

Ganesha's forehead features a third eye, with three lines placed horizontally across the forehead, along with a crescent moon. The depiction of the moon is consistent with one of Ganesha's incarnations, Bhalchandra, or "moon on the forehead." Ganesha's depictions appear in various colors, which stems from the specific text in which he is mentioned. He is commonly seen in the color red. However, his other forms have also shown him in the color white, and his Ekadanta form is often shown in the color blue.

Ganesha's entire appearance holds symbolic meaning as well. The elephant head is a mark of his title as the Remover of Obstacles since elephants remove obstacles in forests to create a path for others to follow. It also stands for the wisdom and intellect one must possess and exercise in life to succeed. Ganesha has large ears, which signify the importance of listening, and his trunk holds everything in existence in the universe.

Etymology

Ganesha's name has its roots in Sanskrit, with the joining of the words *gana* and *isha*, which mean "multitude" and "lord," respectively. Ganas is also the name of the troops of Shiva, and so Ganesha is taken to mean the Lord of the Ganas, which is also noted in his alternate name Ganapati, with *pati* meaning "ruler." Known names of Ganesha's avatars include the following:

- Ganapati
- Vinayaka
- Vighnaraja
- Vighneshwara
- Dvaimatura
- Ganadhipa
- Ekadanta
- Heramba
- Lambodara
- Gajanana

The name Vinayaka is often mentioned in Puranic texts. The eight Ganesha temples in Maharashtra, known collectively as Ashtavinayaka, are named after Vinayaka. The names Vighnaraja and Vighneshwara both signify his title as the Remover of Obstacles, as Vighnaraja means one who removes obstacles and Vighneshwara the one who creates obstacles.

Another common name for Ganesha is taken from the Tamil language. Pillaiyar translates to "noble child." However, taken from the words *pallu* or *pella*, it can also mean elephant tooth or tusk, obviously denoting Ganesha's unique appearance.

Features

Much like other gods of mythology, there are many unique features and attributes associated with Ganesha that signify his role in the cosmic order. These range from the titles he has been given, such as the Remover of Obstacles, to other notable and symbolic features that people should follow to lead wise and successful lives.

Remover of Obstacles

The title of Remover of Obstacles may signify many roles. It may be symbolic, stemming from his elephant form since elephants create paths for others to follow. As Ganesha is also known for his wisdom, the title also signifies his role in creating paths in the spiritual world. However, his role is not simply to remove obstacles. Ganesha places obstacles in the paths of those who deviate from the righteous path or seek to create chaos or evil. This also highlights why Ganesha is celebrated and worshiped at the beginning of any ritual, as invoking him will remove obstacles from people's spiritual path and allow the ritual to continue without any issues.

Symbolically, Ganesha represents the power in each person to overcome the obstacles that face them. Yet his role as the remover of obstacles is not split from his role as the creator of obstacles. In essence, this can mean that moving astray from one's path can create obstacles in life, whereas staying on the right path and practicing wisdom and the use of intellect can keep one away from the challenges of life.

In other interpretations, Ganesha's role as the creator of obstacles is to create perseverance in life. Obstacles allow people to develop strength to face difficult moments in life. As a remover of obstacles, Ganesha practices complete control over disturbing impulses that, if acted on, could lead to the creation of obstacles in one's path. Thus, such obstacles are removed by practicing self-control and by the use of wisdom and strength.

Buddhi (Intelligence)

As the Lord of Letters and Learning, one of Ganesha's most noticeable attributes is his intelligence. Buddhi, or intellect, is a concept that is present in the stories of Ganesha that demonstrate his love and desire for intelligence and cleverness. As such, Ganesha is often referred to as one possessing universal intelligence, or *mahat-tattva*. Among the non-permanent realities that are created and destroyed, intelligence is considered the highest form, and Ganesha, as its possessor, is held in high esteem.

Intelligence in living beings is seen as the culmination of the self, Shiva, and of nature, Parvati. Ganesha, who was born to Shiva and Parvati, is a mixture of their respective traits and can thus possess supreme intelligence. His intellect also relates to his title of Remover of Obstacles, as a great level of intellect is required to carry on through life while removing unnecessary obstructions from one's path.

Along with buddhi, another feature attributed to Ganesha is perfection, siddhi. More specifically, he grants perfection. Hindus believe that one should not pray for materialistic things but rather for intelligence and perfection. Siddhi is most aptly achieved when one receives something before they have a chance to desire it, achieving true perfection. For example, someone who is able to achieve success in life, such as wealth, would not harbor a desire for more money. However, when a desire is expressed and not fulfilled, it shows a lack of siddhi and may also indicate a lack of buddhi. The worship of Ganesha, therefore, brings the qualities of perfection and intellect to the worshiper, who is then able to deal with the challenges of life.

Om

The Om symbol.
https://commons.wikimedia.org/wiki/File:Aum_Om_black.svg

Om is a Hindu mantra with which Ganesha is identified. Ganesha is seen as the personification of the primal sound. Some texts refer to him as the Supreme Being, the culmination of the Trimurti, holding air and fire, the sun and the moon, and the combined three worlds of heaven, earth, and hell. Ganesha, as the possessor or personification of Om, refers to his mastery over all this.

Ganesha is often referred to as Omkara (one with the form of Om) since he manifests it. Many texts and those who practice the worship of Ganesha note that the outline of his body matches the letter that is used to refer to Om. As the personification of all of the cosmos, Ganesha holds great importance and is therefore referred to as a lord equal to the Trimurti.

The mantra that is said to Ganesha is "Om gam ganapataye namaha," which first addresses the primordial sound Om over which Ganesha has complete control and which translates to "wake up." *Gam* and *ganapataye* both refer to Ganesha, and *namaha* offers the reciters salutations and worship to Ganesha. It is also a calling for Ganesha to help the reciter as the remover of obstacles and help them unlock their chakra, or energy centers of the body, and achieve stability in life, over which Ganesha is also lord. The mantra helps tame one's internal anxiety, boosts physical health, and opens the door to wisdom and intellect, which can then lead to better decision-making in life rather than the anxiety one was experiencing.

First Chakra

The Muladhara, or the first chakra, is where Ganesha is believed to reside. This is the root chakra. In the Muladhara, the manifestation and expression of the divine force rest, and Ganesha presides over it. Associated with the earth element, the root chakra is found in one's physical form, namely in the body and in the bones. Ganesha rules the root chakra with his elephant head, his portly belly, and his human form. As the ruler of the Muladhara, Ganesha guides the connection between living beings and their bodies.

The cosmic energies received by the body come through the seven chakras, and the root chakra forms the base of these energies. It is located near the base of the spine and is often associated with the act of secretion. A strong root chakra indicates a strong base, survival, and the ability to stand up for oneself. Without it, one loses their sense and feeling of belonging, creating a weak outlook on life.

Thus, Ganesha is the source of stability, belonging, health, and wealth in the lives of those who master the root chakra. It is also said that Ganesha dwells in the spinal plexus of everybody, which means he is with everyone, offering his support, intellect, and wisdom to those who are able to master the Muladhara. Ganesha also acts as a guide to all the other chakras, thereby guiding the manifestation of one's life and success.

Stories of Ganesha

There are many stories that relate to Ganesha. Many of these signify his attributes, such as his mastery over the root chakra or his wisdom and intellect. Some stories differ in the way they are told. Regardless, they provide insight into the role and significance of Ganesha in the greater cosmic order.

Ganesha's Birth

There are several stories about Ganesha's birth, and many of them seem to vary on certain facts regarding how he came to be and, in particular, how he came to have a single tusk. One story suggests that Ganesha was born from a cloth doll that was brought to life by Parvati's tears after Shiva refused her a child, although a similar story suggests that while Parvati did make Ganesha out of cloth, she asked Shiva to bring him to life.

A more well-known story regarding his birth does not relate to Parvati's desire for a child at all. Instead, Ganesha came to be when Parvati, who wished to bathe without being interrupted by Shiva, conjured Ganesha by kneading the dirt that lay about her and shaping it into a child. The child then came to life. He was assigned to guard the way to where she bathed and to let no one in. When Shiva arrived, he saw a handsome boy who refused him entry. So, he cut the boy's head off in anger. Upon seeing Parvati's sorrow, he vowed to make Ganesha whole again and set off in search of a replacement. The only thing he found was an elephant's head, which was placed on Ganesha's body.

Ganesha is sometimes referred to as only Parvati's son since he was born from one parent. However, he is most commonly referred to as the son of both Parvati and Shiva.

Although there are many stories about how Ganesha only has one tusk, the simplest is that one of his tusks broke off when Shiva placed the elephant's head onto Ganesha's body. Ganesha held on to the broken tusk in one hand. However, other stories differ from this and narrate a different sequence of events that led to the broken tusk.

The Broken Tusk

In one story, Ganesha, as the patron of letters and the arts, sat down to write the *Mahabharata*. This epic poem is one of the longest in existence, and as Ganesha wrote it, the pen he was using broke in his hand. To not let his writing be interrupted, Ganesha is believed to have broken off his tusk and used it as a pen. This sacrifice for an artistic purpose reinforces Ganesha's role as the Lord of Letters and shows his dedication to creating something, even if it came at a personal cost.

Another story presents a different lesson, one of loyalty, and also presents the source of the name Ekadanta. In this story, Shiva asked Ganesha to guard over him while he rested and to allow no stranger to pass through. Ganesha took his post while Shiva slept and stayed true to his task. While Shiva was sleeping, a Brahmin (a warrior) came to visit him, known as Parashuram. Ganesha did not know this warrior and so turned him away. Angered at being refused and also not knowing who Ganesha was, Parashuram began to fight with Ganesha. In his anger, the warrior threw his ax at Ganesha's head, which Ganesha stopped with his tusk, breaking it in the process. Still, he did not let the warrior pass. As for Parashuram, he realized his mistake and felt sorry for what he had done. He asked Shiva for forgiveness, which was granted. This story shows Ganesha's devotion to his assigned duty and his father.

Ganesha's Wisdom

There are many stories that narrate Ganesha's wisdom. One such story begins with Ganesha's conflict with his younger brother Karthikeya, also known as Skanda. The conflict began when the brothers happened upon a unique fruit in the forest. Naturally, each wanted it all to himself and refused to share it with the other. So, they decided to take the matter up with their parents and headed to Mount Kailash.

Shiva immediately recognized the fruit as one possessing great powers; it could grant its eater immortality and great knowledge but could only be consumed by the one with the right to eat it. To resolve their conundrum, Shiva proposed a challenge to the brothers, which they accepted. He asked them both to make three rounds of the world. Whoever finished first would possess the right to consume the fruit of knowledge and immortality.

While Skanda immediately took his pet peacock and began riding around the world, Ganesha took a moment to consider what Shiva had said and realized the trick in the challenge. Instead of attempting to go around all of the created universes, he made three rounds around Shiva and Parvati. Satisfied and impressed by Ganesha's wisdom, Shiva made him the rightful owner of the fruit.

Ganesha's Curse of the Moon

Ganesha's tale about his curse of the moon also relates to his broken tusk. It begins with Ganesha's return journey from a feast thrown by the god of wealth, Kubera. Ganesha had eaten well at the feast, and his mount, a mouse, was having trouble carrying the extra weight. Here, some tales deviate, stating that Ganesha's extra weight made the mouse topple. Other stories suggest that as Ganesha made his journey, a snake crossed his path, and the mouse ran off, causing Ganesha to fall off. His stomach split open, emptying everything he had eaten at the feast.

Ganesha hastily stuffed everything back and took the serpent, tying it around his stomach to hold it in place. However, he heard the moon laughing at him, which angered Ganesha. He broke off one of his tusks and flung it at the moon, which immediately cracked. Ganesha cursed the moon, saying that it would never be whole again. In some versions, Ganesha cursed the moon to never be worshiped during the night of Ganesh Chaturthi. Thus, Ganesha lost his tusk, and the moon earned a permanent crater.

Worship

Thirteenth-century Ganesha statue.
Quadell, CC BY-SA 3.0 <http://creativecommons.org/licenses/by-sa/3.0/>, via Wikimedia Commons; https://commons.wikimedia.org/wiki/File:13th_century_Ganesha_statue.jpg

The worship of Ganesha is not limited to religious events but is a part of daily life for many Hindus. Since he is the Remover of Obstacles, he is often worshiped before the commencement of any undertaking, such as buying a new vehicle, starting a new business, or anything that signifies a new beginning.

Ganesh Chaturthi is an annual festival celebrated in the early fall in honor of Ganesha. The festival lasts ten days, and its beginning is marked by people bringing clay idols of Ganesha. At the end of the ten-day festival, on the day of Anata Chaturdashi, the idols are taken to a suitable body of water and immersed there to allow Ganesha to return home after staying with his devotees for the festival.

Additionally, temple worship of Ganesha is common, but he is portrayed differently based on the temple. He often appears as a subordinate deity (a second deity to the principal deity). In other instances, especially in temples dedicated to him, Ganesha is the principal deity.

Chapter 8: Tales from the *Mahabharata*

The *Mahabharata* is a significant Indian epic and is regarded as one of the longest epic poems ever written. It was initially composed in Sanskrit and is thought to have been written by the sage Vyasa. The epic is an essential component of Indian culture, and literature, art, and philosophy have been impacted by its tales, characters, and lessons for centuries.

The *Mahabharata* describes a war between two branches of the Kuru dynasty for control of the Kuru Kingdom. The five Pandava brothers' conflict with their Kaurava cousins, who seized control of their kingdom, is the central theme of the story. The eldest brother, Yudhishthira, is in charge of the Pandavas, who are regarded as the story's main characters. Duryodhana, the eldest brother, is in charge of the Kauravas.

The epic is supposedly set in the ancient Kuru Kingdom, which is said to be in what is now northern India's Haryana. The Kuru dynasty and its kings, including King Shantanu and his son Bhishma, are introduced at the beginning of the story. The plot then follows the Pandavas' lives and their conflicts with the Kauravas, which ultimately result in a terrible battle.

The *Mahabharata* explores a variety of philosophical and ethical topics in addition to telling the tale of a conflict between two families. Discussions of dharma (goodness), karma (activities and their results), and *moksha* (deliverance from the cycle of life and death) are all included in the epic. A discussion between the warrior Arjuna and his charioteer Krishna makes up the Bhagavad Gita, which is a chapter of the *Mahabharata*. One of the most important Hindu teachings is the dialogue between Arjuna and Krishna, as it examines a number of spiritual and ethical ideas.

There are other storylines and subplots in the *Mahabharata* as well. The tale of Nala and Damayanti is one such tale that explores the concepts of love and trust. Another well-known story is the tale of Savitri and Satyavan, which is about loyalty and devotion.

The *Mahabharata* is not only a religious book; it is also a work of culture and history. It sheds light on the habits, traditions, and ideals of ancient Indian society. The epic depicts the numerous roles that women play in society, especially the formidable and powerful figure of Draupadi, the Pandava king's wife. The value of family, allegiance, and honor in Indian culture is also portrayed in it.

Satyavati and the Kuru Dynasty

King Shantanu and Satyavati.
https://commons.wikimedia.org/wiki/File:Santanu,_a_king_of_Hastinapura_in_the_Mahabharata,_saw_a_beautiful_woman_on_the_banks_of_the_river_Ganga.jpg

An essential figure in the epic *Mahabharata* was Satyavati. Born to be a fisherwoman, Satyavati was renowned for her extraordinary beauty and charisma. Her life is an amazing story of love and devotion.

Satyavati was the daughter of a fisherman named Dasharaja. Because of her father's occupation, she was given the name Matsyagandha, which translates to "one who smells of fish." Nevertheless, she was endowed with great beauty and grace despite coming from a lowly background.

One day, Satyavati drew Parashara's attention while she was escorting the great sage across the river. He asked her to spend the night with him. Initially reluctant, Satyavati consented on the condition that he would make her smell good forever. She got her wish.

Satyavati gave birth to a boy after their night together, and he was given the name Vyasa. Vyasa would later become a famous sage and pen the *Mahabharata*.

After some time, Satyavati wed King Shantanu of Hastinapur, who was captivated by her beauty and elegance. But they faced difficulties in their marriage. Chitrangada and Vichitravirya were the names of Satyavati and Shantanu's two children. Vichitravirya became the only heir to the kingdom after Chitrangada's early death.

When Vichitravirya was of marriageable age, Satyavati made arrangements for his union with the king of Kashi's daughters, Ambika and Ambalika. However, Vichitravirya passed very quickly after the wedding and left no heir. As a result, there was no one to take the throne, which caused a crisis in the country.

Satyavati requested the assistance of Vyasa, her child from her union with Parashara, to preserve the survival of the Kuru dynasty. She asked him to have children with Ambika and Ambalika so that the Kuru dynasty's legacy would live on. Satyavati gave Vyasa the order to conceive Ambika while she was in her reproductive cycle. When they first met, Ambika's discomfort with Vyasa's dark skin caused her to close her eyes. She thus gave birth to a robust, blind boy who went on to become the ancestor of the Kauravas. Satyavati deemed his condition to be inappropriate for a monarch, and she requested that Vyasa perform a similar act with her younger daughter-in-law, Ambalika. But when Ambalika saw Vyasa, she grew frightened and gave birth to a thin infant. Thus, Pandu, the pallid one, and Dhritarashtra, the blind monarch, entered the universe.

Satyavati was essential to the founding and survival of the Kuru dynasty. Her descendants carried on her heritage by taking part in the epic battle of Kurukshetra.

Pandu and Dhritarashtra

In the *Mahabharata*, the two brothers named Pandu and Dhritarashtra had a significant impact on the events that led to the War of Kurukshetra.

Dhritarashtra was Pandu's older brother and was born blind. Due to his disability, Pandu was chosen to rule Hastinapura, the Kuru kingdom's capital.

Duryodhana, the major adversary of the *Mahabharata*, was one of Dhritarashtra's one hundred sons. He was married to Gandhari, who blindfolded herself so she could understand her husband's pain.

Dhritarashtra.
Ramanarayanadatta astri, CC0, via Wikimedia Commons;
https://commons.wikimedia.org/wiki/File:Dhritrashtra.jpg

Pandu, the younger brother, ruled for a time. One day, he was in the forest, enjoying the wildlife and the sounds of nature. All of a sudden, he heard the noise of a wild animal. He shot an arrow toward the sound, hitting a sage who had turned into a deer to engage in lovemaking. He curses Pandu, saying that he will die if he ever has sex. Pandu went into the forest with his wives, leaving the throne to Dhritarashtra.

The Conflict between the Pandava Brothers and Their Cousins, the Kauravas

The battle between the Pandavas and Kauravas.
https://commons.wikimedia.org/wiki/File:The_Pandava_brothers%27_nephew_Abhimanyu_battles_the_Kaurava_brother_Duhshasana,_from_a_manuscript_of_the_Mahabharata.jpg

The greatest fight in the *Mahabharata* is between the five Pandava brothers and their relatives, the Kauravas. The rivalry between the two lineages of the Kuru dynasty, which were descendants of the fabled King Kuru, was the cause of the conflict. The battle is a complicated tale encompassing a number of elements, including resentment, greed, pride, and power.

King Pandu was the father of the five Pandavas. But how did Pandu have five sons if he would die after having intercourse? A wise sage accepted their mother Kunti's yearning to call upon the gods' favor to have children. She invoked the gods Dharmaraja, Vayu, and Indra to give birth to her three sons, Yudhishthira, Bhima, and Arjuna. Madri,

Pandu's other wife, prayed to the Ashvinis (Hindu twin gods that are associated with medicine, health, dawn, as well as the sciences) to help her conceive her two sons, Nakula and Sahadeva. Pandu eventually had sex with Madri and died soon afterward. Madri, ashamed at what had happened, committed suicide, leaving Kunti to raise the five sons on her own.

Kunti raised them in the capital alongside their cousins, the Kauravas. However, the eldest Kaurava, Duryodhana, refused to accept them as his family. He hated the Pandavas, and this hatred spread to the other Kauravas.

Several schemes to hurt or kill the Pandavas were developed by Duryodhana, which included poisoning their food, drowning them in a river, and burning them in a house of wax. Duryodhana believed the fire had killed them, but the brothers lived, having been forewarned of the plot.

News of the Pandavas' existence eventually reached their uncle's ears, and he welcomed them back to the kingdom with open arms. But Duryodhana, who was now the recognized heir, did not want them to return, as he knew questions about inheritance would be raised. Dhritarashtra knew it would not be right to cut the Pandavas out entirely, so he kept the capital and its surrounding lands for himself and his son and gave desolate lands to the Pandavas.

It was challenging, but the Pandavas were able to build their kingdom into something amazing. Duryodhana, who was greatly influenced by his uncle, Shakuni, decided to play a dice game with his eldest cousin, Yudhishthira. The dice Duryodhana used was magical, allowing him to win every time. First, he cheated Yudhishthira out of his wealth and kingdom. Then, Yudhishthira bet his brothers, himself, and even his wife, making the family slaves to Duryodhana. in which he cheated and gained the kingdom.

Duryodhana humiliated the Pandavas, causing Dhritarashtra to finally intervene, giving everything back to the Pandavas. But Duryodhana threw a fit and threatened to kill himself if he wasn't allowed to play one more game with the Pandavas. This time, the loser would be sent to live in the forest for twelve years and spend the thirteenth year in disguise. If their cover was blown during the thirteenth year, the cycle would begin again. Thanks to the magical dice, Duryodhana won, and the Pandavas were exiled.

The Pandavas spent their time wisely, gathering supplies and an army to take the capital by force if needed. When their time was up, they returned to Hastinapura, asking for their former kingdom back. Duryodhana, who was now the king, was unwilling to divide his kingdom. Krishna intervened, asking for Duryodhana to give up five villages, but he still refused. A war was unavoidable. According to tradition, millions of troops and fighters perished during the eighteen-day Kurukshetra War, which also claimed the lives of some significant *Mahabharata* figures, including Bhishma, Drona, Karna, and many others. The Pandavas ultimately triumphed, and Yudhishthira was anointed king of Hastinapura.

The struggle between good and evil and the victory of dharma (righteousness) over adharma (unrighteousness) are represented by the war between the Pandavas and the Kauravas. The narrative is also full of lessons, and it has served as an example and a source of inspiration for individuals of all ages.

The Bhagavad Gita

A seven-hundred-verse Hindu scripture known as the Bhagavad Gita is included in the *Mahabharata*. Many believe it is a manual for spiritual and moral conduct and see it as one of Hinduism's most significant works.

Arjuna, a warrior prince, and Lord Krishna, his charioteer, converse in the Bhagavad Gita. Arjuna is prepared to lead his army against his own relatives in the struggle for control of the kingdom. When Arjuna recognizes members of his family and friends among the enemy, he is struck with sorrow and uncertainty and loses all motivation to fight.

According to the Bhagavad Gita, Arjuna was overcome with contradictory feelings and skepticism about the rationale for the war on the eve of the War of Kurukshetra. He was considering the possibility of engaging in combat with and killing his own family members and teachers and was debating on how to proceed. Lord Krishna, an incarnation of the Hindu god Vishnu, was Arjuna's charioteer and companion. Arjuna confided his worries and uncertainties to him.

In response, Lord Krishna gave a speech known as the Bhagavad Gita, which contains some of the most profound philosophical ideas. Krishna imparted to Arjuna the nature of the self, the universe, and the divine, as well as yoga's potential for achieving nirvana. Krishna further emphasized that Arjuna's job as a warrior was to battle and carry out his dharma, regardless of the result.

Arjuna was advised by Krishna to execute his deeds as an act of worship rather than becoming emotionally connected to the results of what happened. He emphasized that death was merely a change from one form to another and that the actual self was everlasting and indestructible.

Lord Krishna inspired Arjuna to engage in combat with bravery, tenacity, and objectivity. After overcoming his fears and trepidations, Arjuna bravely took part in the War of Kurukshetra. The Bhagavad Gita has since become one of Hinduism's most revered literary masterpieces, and its message of esoteric wisdom has inspired millions of people all over the world.

Karna

One of the most fascinating narratives in the *Mahabharata* is the tale of Karna's birth. The myth claims that Kunti, the mother of the Pandavas, gave birth to Karna before she wed Pandu.

As the story goes, Kunti was intrigued and anxious to test the power of the boon she was granted by the sage Durvasa. She wanted to try out this ability to summon any god and have a child with them.

Kunti made the decision to test the boon's effectiveness one day. She requested a son from Surya, the sun god, and gave birth to Karna. However, Kunti abandoned the infant Karna in a basket and floated him down a river out of fear that having a child out of wedlock would have negative social repercussions.

Adhiratha and Radha, a childless couple, ultimately discovered the basket and took the infant in as their own. They gave him the name Vasusena. The child grew to become a proficient archer and warrior. Vasusena had a natural knack for weapons, and Dhritarashtra soon learned of his abilities.

Vasusena discovered his true identity when he grew older and realized that he was Karna, Kunti's abandoned son. The news originally devastated him, but he soon made up his mind to prove himself a warrior and win the admiration and respect of his fellow soldiers.

There were difficulties on Karna's path to fame and glory. Due to his humble origins, he experienced prejudice and derision from some quarters, but he was unfazed and devoted to his training. Karna swiftly outperformed many of his contemporaries in terms of his ability to use a bow and arrow, and he became known as a legendary warrior.

Later, during the War of Kurukshetra, Karna turned into a crucial ally of the Kauravas, the Pandavas' cousins. He bravely fought for them, but his allegiance to the Kaurava prince and his companion, Duryodhana, brought about his demise. Karna was ultimately beaten in a brutal battle by Arjuna, one of the Pandava brothers, despite his remarkable bravery and talents.

Death of Karna.
https://commons.wikimedia.org/wiki/File:Death_of_Karna.jpg

The Tale of Drona

Drona was renowned for his prowess as a warrior, mentor, and friend. His deeds and way of life were crucial to the circumstances that set off the War of Kurukshetra.

Drona is the revered teacher for both the Kauravas and the Pandavas throughout the epic. He is a significant counselor and fighter in the narrative. Drona is acknowledged as the son of the sage Bharadvaja, although Drona was not born to a mother. Bharadvaja sees a beautiful apsara (somewhat similar to a nymph) and is overcome with lust. He spills his seed into a pot, giving birth to Drona.

Bharadvaja teaches Drona and Prince Drupada at his hermitage. He teaches the children knowledge of the mystical weapons known as astras and superior military techniques. Drona and Drupada become good friends, and Drona promises to help Drupada for the rest of his life. Eventually, Drupada gains the throne of Panchala, while Drona adopts a simple lifestyle as a wise man and teacher. The chapter also introduces Ashwatthama, Drona's son.

Drona was known for his rigorous teaching methods, and he evaluated his students' loyalty in addition to their skills. He was the one behind shaping Arjuna into a master archer and a committed defender of morality. Arjuna received criticism from other pupils for being given preference, but Drona defended his decision by putting the other students through a loyalty test. Only Arjuna demonstrated everlasting loyalty.

Arjuna was taught the art of fighting by Drona, including how to use the Brahmastra sword. He also taught Prince Duryodhana how to become a proficient warrior and how to destroy Arjuna's brothers, the Pandavas. Drona supported Duryodhana and his army during the War of Kurukshetra. He was an extremely tough opponent, and his proficiency with the Brahmastra, combined with his warrior prowess, made him practically unbeatable.

However, Drona resisted Duryodhana's attempt to use him to murder the Pandavas because he understood that it went against his role as a teacher. A teacher should not injure their own pupils. When Duryodhana detected his reluctance, he deceived Drona into thinking that his son Ashwatthama had been killed in combat. Drona unleashed the Brahmastra in a moment of fury and despair, causing extensive damage and devastation.

Drona was ultimately defeated by the Pandavas in combat through guile and trickery. Both sides lamented his passing since he was so well liked and recognized for his abilities and moral character.

The story of Drona in the *Mahabharata* serves as a warning of the perils of arrogance, retaliation, and mistaken allegiance. It demonstrates how even the most knowledgeable and wise can succumb to their emotions and forget their true calling in life.

Conclusion

The *Mahabharata*, an important ancient Indian epic, describes a dynastic conflict between two branches of a royal dynasty. In addition to providing insight into ancient Indian civilization, it also explores a variety of philosophical and ethical questions.

Hindi, Tamil, Telugu, and Bengali are only a few of the languages in which the epic has been translated. Its characters and tales are still present in Indian popular culture, and they have served as an inspiration for several plays, films, and television shows. The themes of dharma, karma, and *moksha* continue to be important in Hinduism, and its teachings have also influenced Indian philosophy and spirituality.

Chapter 9: Tales from the *Ramayana*

The *Ramayana* is the other important Hindu epic. This Sanskrit epic is largely attributed to Maharishi Valmiki, a legendary poet of his time, who composed it sometime after 300 BCE. The epic consists of over twenty-four thousand shlokas, or couplets, spread out over seven books.

The *Ramayana* follows the life and adventures of Rama during his exile. The epic holds great value in Hindu and Buddhist traditions. Rama's story illustrates what an ideal society ought to look like, from the formation of the state to its people. The narration of history, *itihasa*, is combined with morals and lessons on human life.

Who Were Rama and Sita?

Rama and Sita.
Ayan Gupta, CC BY-SA 3.0 <https://creativecommons.org/licenses/by-sa/3.0>, via Wikimedia Commons; https://commons.wikimedia.org/wiki/File:Ram-Sita.jpg

The protagonist, Rama, is an avatar of the god Vishnu. Rama was the son of Dasharatha, the king of the Kosala Kingdom. After Rama's marriage to Sita, his life was marked by challenges and tribulations that began with his exile from his rightful kingdom. Rama is known to have three brothers: Lakshmana, Bharata, and Shatrughna.

As mentioned, Rama was the incarnation of Vishnu in human form. Vishnu reportedly took on the responsibility of dealing with Ravana, who had spread chaos throughout the world. He took this vow when the demigods turned to Brahma for help against the demon. The texts describe Rama's early life and upbringing as virtuous. Rama was polite and kind and had a reserved personality. He was taught the Vedas, the Vedangas (which aid in the study and understanding of the Vedas), and martial arts.

As well as the female protagonist of the *Ramayana*, Sita was the wife of Rama and is considered the human incarnation of the goddess Lakshmi. She is known as the daughter of the earth goddess Bhumi but was brought up by the king of Videha, Janaka, as his adopted daughter. She is said to have been found in a furrowed field by the king, who took her in and raised her as his own.

Sita and Rama married after Rama won a bow-stringing contest. Sita chose him from a group of eligible suitors. Sita also chose to go to Ayodhya, Rama's birthplace, with him to spend their lives together. She accompanied him in his later exile. Much of the *Ramayana* is focused on Rama's efforts to retrieve Sita when she was taken by Ravana. The epic also features other characters central to the story.

Hanuman

Statue of Hanuman.
MatrixInDWD, CC BY-SA 4.0 <https://creativecommons.org/licenses/by-sa/4.0>, via Wikimedia Commons; https://commons.wikimedia.org/wiki/File:Statue_of_Lord_Hanuman_at_Dharwad.jpg

A central character, Hanuman is a divine ape god appointed to be Rama's companion. In addition to being an avatar of Shiva, Hanuman is regarded as the son of Vayu, the god of the wind. Hanuman is believed to have been born to Anjana and Kesari but is regarded as the spiritual son of Vayu due to the role the wind god played in his birth. He was born as an ape due to a curse placed on his mother by a sage whom she had angered.

According to legend, King Dasharatha was performing a ritual to have children, during which he was given a pudding by the gods to give to his three wives. This pudding allowed his wives to bear sons. Some of this pudding was taken away by a bird. The wind pushed the bird into the outstretched hands of Kesara, who had been praying to be blessed with a child. Hanuman was thus born by the grace of Vayu.

Ravana

Statue of Ravana.
Indi Samarajiva, CC BY 2.0 <https://creativecommons.org/licenses/by/2.0>, via Wikimedia Commons; https://commons.wikimedia.org/wiki/File:Ravana_Statue.jpg

Ravana acts as the antagonist in the *Ramayana*. He is the multi-headed demon-king of Lanka. While a well-learned scholar, Ravana is portrayed as an evil character who spreads strife and kidnaps the wife of Rama. Born to Vishrava and Kaikesi as their eldest son, Ravana is known to be devoted to Shiva. He is often portrayed as having ten heads, although he is sometimes shown with nine; in those tales, he cut off a head in devotion to Shiva.

Ravana's scholarly pursuits include the authorship of *Ravana Samhita*, a book on astrology, and he also was knowledgeable in medicine and politics. He was a master of the veena. Brahma also granted Ravana a boon: the gift of immortality, allowing him invincibility from the hands of all creations of Brahma except humans. Ravana received weapons, a chariot, and the power of shapeshifting from Brahma in response to the sacrifices Ravana made.

Exile to the Forest

After Rama and Sita were married, the two traveled to Ayodhya to spend their lives together. At this time, King Dasharatha, who had been growing old, was considering giving the crown to his eldest son. This proved a popular decision in the court and among his subjects, who all approved of the quiet and kind Rama as their king. But this decision did not sit well with Kaikeyi, the second wife of the king and stepmother to Rama. In Rama's absence, after the king had made the decision of who should ascend his throne, the queen reminded him of his promise that he had made to her a while ago to comply with any one thing that she asked.

The king remembered and was bound by his promise, so he agreed to hear her request. The queen demanded that Rama be exiled to the forest of Dandaka for fourteen years, giving her son, Bharata, enough time to become king and gain the people's favor. This request was not well received by any of the royal family. Even Bharata opposed his mother's request. However, Rama wanted his father to fulfill the promise he had made to his wife, stating that he had no wish for a throne or other material trappings of the earthly world.

Against the wishes of others, including his father and brother, Rama chose to go into exile as his stepmother had requested after discussing the matter with Sita. While Dasharatha grieved at Kaikeyi's request, and even though Bharata asked his brother not to go, he undertook this journey, stating that time passes quickly. As he was leaving, Bharata promised Rama that he would rule the kingdom in his name until he returned. When Rama and Sita left to go into exile, they were followed by Lakshmana, who accompanied Rama out of brotherly love.

The Period of Exile

After Rama and Sita left the Kingdom of Kosala, they spent some time on the banks of the River Mandakini in a region called Chitrakoot, located on the borders of modern-day Madhya Pradesh and Uttar Pradesh. During this time, Rama and Sita stayed with a sage called Vasishtha. Rama also met Shabari, a devotee of his, who offered her own berries to Rama to eat, first testing each one to ensure it was sweet.

The following years of exile passed as Rama and Sita roamed through the forests and lived with various sages, such as Atri. The two lived a quiet and simple life in the wild, offering protection from demons to those being harassed and persecuted and attempting to live humbly without depending on the material comforts of the world. The two lived this way for the next ten years until Ravana turned his attention toward them.

Sita's Abduction

After ten years of exile, Rama and Sita settled on the banks of the River Godavari in a place called Panchavati. This region was plagued by demons, and one such demon brought chaos to Rama's and Sati's lives. Surpanakha, who is said to be the sister of Ravana and might have been sent by him, caught sight of Rama and was infatuated with him. She attempted to seduce him, but her advances were rejected.

Infuriated, Surpanakha threatened Sati, and in response, Lakshmana cut off her nose and ears. These events reached Ravana, who sought revenge on Rama for the treatment of his sister. He tracked Rama and Sati down, but when he laid eyes on Sati, he was enchanted by her beauty and began to hatch a plan to obtain her.

He ordered his servant, Maricha, to disguise himself as a golden deer. This deer was meant to lure Rama and Lakshmana away from Sita. However, Rama and Lakshmana did not forget Sita in their haste. Lakshmana drew a protective circle around Sita, forbidding her to leave it until the two returned. Ravana knew about Sita's kindness, though. He appeared before her as an old beggar, asking for food. In pity, Sita stepped out of the circle, and Ravana was able to grab her, throwing her in his flying chariot. Hearing her screams for help, a passing bird, Jatayu, tried to save her, only to have its wings cut off by Ravana. In the hopes of rescue, Sita threw down her necklace so Rama could find her.

The Defeat of Ravana

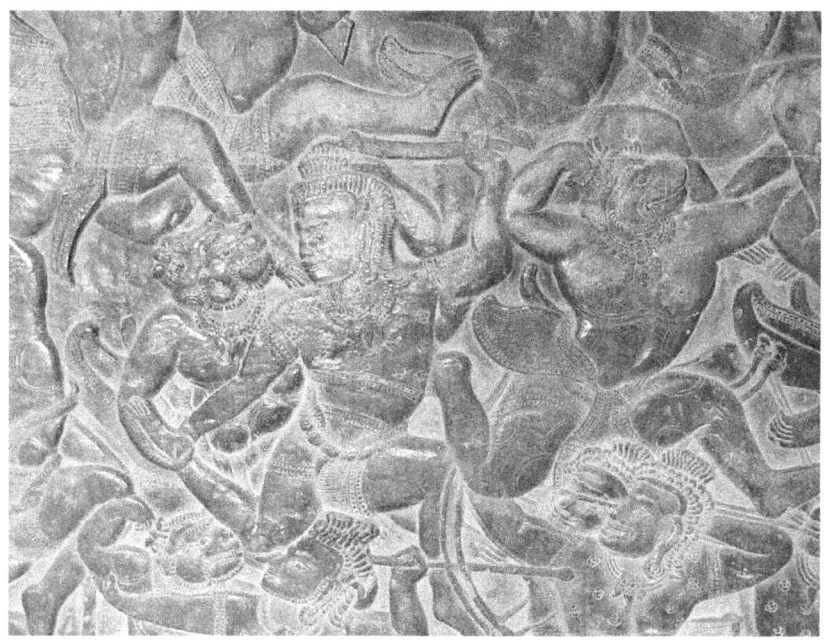

The Battle of Lanka at Angkor Wat.
Photo Dharma from Penang, Malaysia, CC BY 2.0 <https://creativecommons.org/licenses/by/2.0>, via Wikimedia Commons; https://commons.wikimedia.org/wiki/File:Angkor_Wat_-_103_Battle_of_Lanka_(8581635902).jpg

When Rama and Lakshmana returned, they learned of Sita's kidnapping from Jatayu. The two immediately set out in search of Sita, but they despaired since they had no means to travel swiftly and nothing to aid them in their journey. They had no resources to fight Ravana and free Sita. Traveling south, they met the sage Shabari, who led them to Hanuman.

Lakshmana and Rama headed to the Monkey Kingdom of Vanara to meet Hanuman, who was a devotee of Rama and an ape hero. Hanuman was minister to Sugriva, who had been banished from his rightful throne of Kishkindha by his brother Vali. To earn Sugriva's support and trust, Rama and Lakshmana decided to help him by killing Vali and establishing him as the head of his kingdom. In exchange, Sugriva promised to help rescue Sita.

However, Sugriva became enmeshed in his newly regained kingdom and forgot his promises to Rama. Lakshmana was angered at the treachery, and in his rage, he threatened to destroy the ape citadel over which Sugriva reigned. But before this could happen, Tara, the former ape queen and wife of Vali, intervened. She convinced Sugriva to stand by his word.

Thus, search parties were sent out to the north, east, west, and south. Three parties came back bearing no news, having heard nothing of Ravana or Sita. The southern party, led by Angada and Hanuman, learned from a vulture, a brother to Jatayu, that Sita had been taken by Ravana to the land of Lanka, which refers to modern-day Sri Lanka. Ravana had attempted to convince Sita to become his consort, but she repeatedly refused his advances.

Hanuman's Heroics

Armed with the knowledge of Sita's location, Hanuman took the lead, taking on the form of a gargantuan ape and leaping across the sea to Lanka. His journey to Lanka was beset with tests and challenges, including a demon who challenged his abilities and a mountain that offered him rest and comfort. Yet Hanuman proved himself time and time again. When he finally reached Lanka, he was met by the demon Lankini, who was charged with the protection of Lanka.

Lankini had seen the end of Lanka should she fall. Hanuman was able to defeat her, thereby gaining entry into Lanka. Once inside, Hanuman spied on Ravana and was able to track down where Sita was being held. He also witnessed Ravana terrorizing and threatening her in an attempt to convince her to become his wife.

When Ravana and his demon guards left, Hanuman was able to reach out to Sita. He assured her that Rama was still alive, offering his signet ring as proof of her husband's existence. He then offered to carry her back to Rama. Sita refused, stating that such a rescue must be done by Rama in order to avenge her. As proof of her being alive, Sita gave Hanuman her comb to give to Rama.

Before Hanuman left to inform Rama of what had transpired between him and Sita, he chose to create trouble for Ravana. Hanuman wreaked havoc in Lanka by uprooting trees, destroying buildings, and killing many of Ravana's soldiers. In order to meet with Ravana, Hanuman allowed himself to be captured. When he was before Ravana, he demanded that the demon release Sita. In response, Ravana set Hanuman's tail on fire. Hanuman escaped, leaping from roof to roof and setting Ravana's citadel on fire. He then returned to Kishkindha to deliver the news to Rama.

The War between Rama and Ravana

Following Hanuman's return, Rama and Lakshmana began to prepare their armies to march to Lanka. At the shore of the southern sea, they were joined by Ravana's brother, Vibhishana, who sought vengeance against Ravana for throwing him out of the kingdom. As the armies sought to cross the sea, the apes Nila and Nala created a floating bridge made from stones that had Rama's name written on them. These stones were blessed and could not sink. In other narrations, the curse of a sage prevented anything thrown by the two from sinking.

After the armies crossed the sea and entered Lanka, a long war began. Lakshmana was grievously injured by a powerful weapon shot by Ravana's son Indrajit. In response, Hanuman assumed his gigantic ape form again and leaped from Lanka to the Himalayas in search of an herb that could cure Lakshmana. When he was unable to find it, he took the entire mountain and brought it back to Lanka. The war finally came to an end when Rama was able to kill Ravana. He put Vibhishana on the throne.

Rama was finally able to free Sita, and upon their meeting, he assured her that the dishonor of her abduction had been avenged. However, Sita's return was not met with joy by all. Many from Rama's kingdom raised questions about Sita's purity. In response, Rama sent Sita away, telling her to find some other shelter. Seeking to prove her fidelity, Sita asked Lakshmana to build her a pyre. Praying to the god of fire, Agni, Sita walked into the raging fire. Agni appeared from the flames, carrying Sita in his arms, thus proving her purity. Sita was then joyfully reunited with Rama.

Rama's Reign of Ayodhya

Following the end of their exile, Rama and Sita returned to Ayodhya, accompanied by Lakshmana and Hanuman. There, the two were crowned king and queen, yet their days of prosperity were numbered. Despite Sita's proof of her purity by walking through fire, Rama's subjects again questioned her loyalty since she had resided in another man's house. While Rama was furious with the allegations, he was forced to send Sita into exile into the forest while she was pregnant.

Sita would give birth to her twins, Lava and Kusha, while in exile. When the brothers grew up, they engaged in war with the Kingdom of Kosala, defeating the entire army of Ayodhya, as well as Lakshmana, Shatrughna, and Bharata. They even took Hanuman captive. It was not until Rama arrived that the two brothers were defeated and taken back to Ayodhya, where they attempted to convince the people of Sita's sacrifice. It was only when Sita herself emerged that Rama realized the captured brothers were his own sons.

Sita still faced challenges to her character. Overwhelmed, she declared that the earth should swallow her whole if she was pure, and sure enough, the earth beneath her feet opened up and swallowed her.

The rest of Rama's rule was uneventful. Eventually, he, along with his brothers, left the world. He returned to his true form as Vishnu and was reunited with Sita, who had already taken her true form as Lakshmi.

Conclusion

Indian mythology forms a significant part of the religious belief system in India and continues to impact the cultural practices of many regions in Southeast Asia. In addition to contributing to religious beliefs and practices, it also had a significant impact on art, poetry, drama, and other works of fiction. It has inspired other forms of artistic expression, including unique dance forms, such as Kathak and Bharatnatyam, which incorporate many features of Hindu mythology in their movements. Indian mythology has also inspired traditional music, such as music created with the sitar and tabla.

Hindu mythology has influenced many cultures outside of India. The Indonesian currency, for example, depicts Ganesha, showing the impact of Hinduism on the country's history and culture. Even video games, such as the *Indus Battle Royale*, images of which were played in Times Square in New York City in 2022, depict Ganesha and other aspects of Hindu mythology. There is even a statue of Shiva outside the CERN building in Switzerland.

The concept of Indo-futurism has taken the world by storm. The concept visualizes a futuristic world through science fiction, art, and music where the Indus Valley civilization inhabits another planet rather than going extinct. This idea features many elements from Hindu mythology and spirituality, such as showing Jatayu with phoenix wings. While the concept itself was created to challenge India's colonial history and the Western views of the future, it has become an increasingly common sight in popular culture.

While portraying perhaps the lesser-known aspects of Hindu mythology, this concept attempts to show Indian mythology as the beacon of the future. In essence, Indo-futurism provides a peek into the future through music, art, film, television, science fiction, and even video games and brings light to the mythology that was misplaced in the annals of colonial history.

We hope you enjoyed this introductory look at Indian mythology, and we encourage you to take a look at our bibliography to continue learning about this fascinating aspect of Indian culture.

Here's another book by Enthralling History that you might like

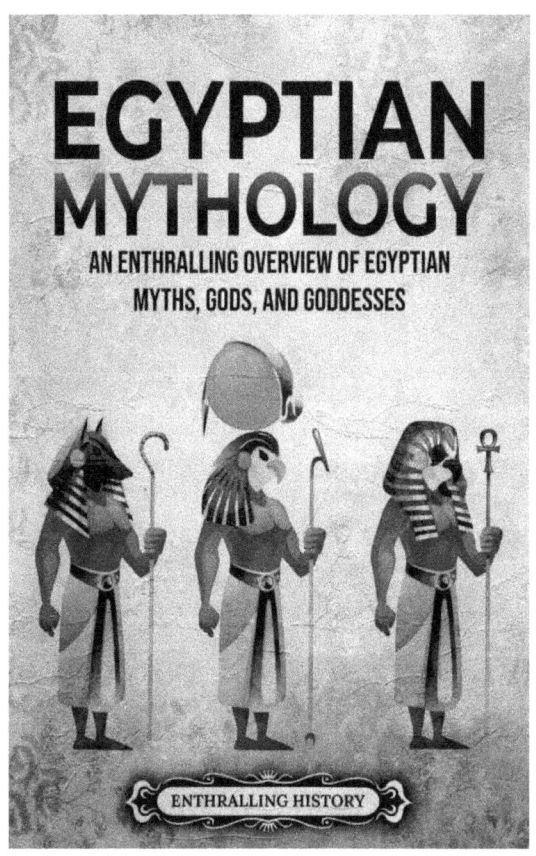

Free limited time bonus

Stop for a moment. We have a free bonus set up for you. The problem is this: we forget 90% of everything that we read after 7 days. Crazy fact, right? Here's the solution: we've created a printable, 1-page pdf summary for this book that you're reading now. All you have to do to get your free pdf summary is to go to the following website:

https://livetolearn.lpages.co/enthrallinghistory/

Once you do, it will be intuitive. Enjoy, and thank you!

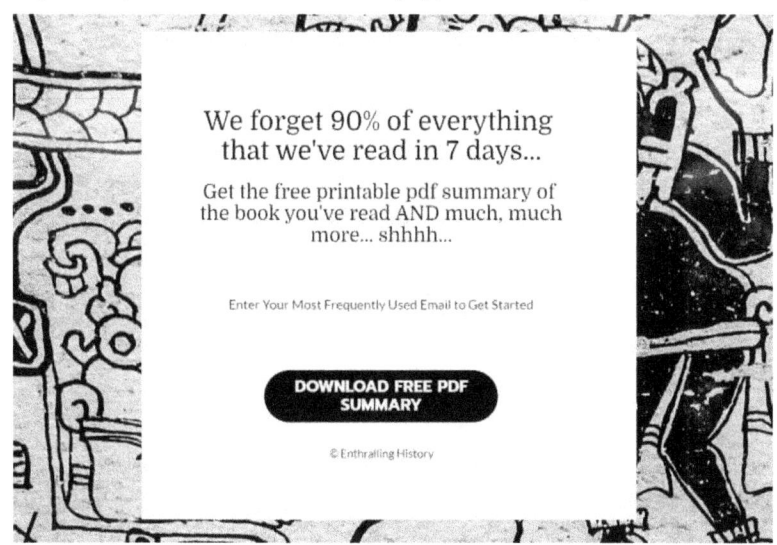

Bibliography

Britannica, The Editors of Encyclopedia. "Durga | Goddess, Personality, & Story." *Encyclopedia Britannica*, 2023, https://www.britannica.com/topic/Durga.

Britannica, The Editors of Encyclopedia. "Lakshmi | Hindu deity | Britannica." *Encyclopedia Britannica*, 5 April 2023, https://www.britannica.com/topic/Lakshmi.

The British Library. "Princess Sita's Kidnap - The *Ramayana*." *The British Library*, 2022, https://www.bl.uk/learning/cult/inside/*Ramayana*stories/sitaskidnap/sitaskidnap.html.

Brown, Norman W. "Theories of Creation in the Rig Veda." *Journal of the American Oriental Society*, vol. 85, no. 1, 1965, pp. 23-25. *JSTOR*, https://doi.org/10.2307/597699.

Burke, Elisabeth. "Vedic Creation Hymn." *Humanities LibreTexts*, 5 May 2021, https://human.libretexts.org/Bookshelves/Religious_Studies/Scriptures_of_the_Worlds_Religions_(Burke)/02%3A_Hindu_Scriptures/2.01%3A_Vedic_Creation_Hymn.

Cartwright, Mark, et al. "Lakshmi." *World History Encyclopedia*, 14 August 2015, https://www.worldhistory.org/Lakshmi/.

Cartwright, Mark, et al. "Saraswati." *World History Encyclopedia*, 25 November 2015, https://www.worldhistory.org/Sarasvati/.

Chandran, Nyshka. "An 'unapologetically Indian' universe." *BBC*, 9 January 2023, https://www.bbc.com/culture/article/20230106-the-ancient-indian-myths-resonating-now.

"CHAPTER IX. THE PURĀNIC ACCOUNT OF THE CREATION." *Hindu Mythology: Vedic and Purānic*, by William Joseph Wilkins, D K Printworld (P) Limited, 2003.

Doniger, Wendy. "Ganesha | Meaning, Symbolism, & Facts | Britannica." *Encyclopedia Britannica*, 1 April 2023, https://www.britannica.com/topic/Ganesha.

Doniger, Wendy. "Parvati, Hindu deity." *Encyclopedia Britannica*, 1 April 2023, https://www.britannica.com/topic/Parvati.

Doniger, Wendy. "Purana | Hindu literature | Britannica." *Encyclopedia Britannica*, 2022, https://www.britannica.com/topic/Purana.

Emory University. "Maa Saraswati | Emory | Michael C. Carlos Museum." *the Carlos Museum*, 2013, https://carlos.emory.edu/maa-saraswati.

"Ganesh and Root Chakra, Lord Ganpati Relation with Muladhara Chakra – Rudraksha Centre." *Rudraksha Ratna*, 2020, https://www.rudraksha-ratna.com/articles/ganesh-the-god-of-root-chakra.

The Goddess Garden. "The Hindu Goddess Parvati." *The Goddess Garden*, 9 November 2018, https://thegoddessgarden.com/the-hindu-goddess-parvati/.

Heaphy, Linda. "The Hindu God Ganesh - Who is this Elephant Headed Fellow Anyway?" *Kashgar*, 2020, https://kashgar.com.au/blogs/gods-goddesses/the-hindu-god-ganesh-who-is-this-elephant-headed-deity-anyway.

HISTORY. "Hinduism - Origins, Facts & Beliefs." *HISTORY*, 2019, https://www.history.com/topics/religion/hinduism.

Liu, H. "Multiverse (Religion)." *Scholarly Community Encyclopedia*, Encyclopedia MDPI, 21 November 2022, https://encyclopedia.pub/entry/35469.

Lotus Sculpture. "Ganesha Hindu God, the Remover Obstacles, Learn About Ganesh." *Lotus Sculpture*, 2022, https://www.lotussculpture.com/ganesha-hindu-god-ganapati-elephant-meaning-symbolism.html.

Marin, Kimi. "Your Base Power: Ganesha and the First Chakra - Beyogi." *beYogi*, 22 June 2015, https://beyogi.com/your-base-power-ganesha-first-chakra/.

Mathur, Priyanshi. "Ganesh Chaturthi 2019: 10 Lesser-Known Short Stories of Bal Ganesha You Need to Know." *Indiatimes.com*, 9 October 2019, https://www.indiatimes.com/trending/social-relevance/ganesh-chaturthi-short-stories-374788.html.

Murphy, Anne. "*Ramayana*." *Asia Society*, 2020, https://asiasociety.org/education/*Ramayana*.

New World Encyclopedia. "Parvati." *New World Encyclopedia*, 2023, https://www.newworldencyclopedia.org/entry/Parvati.

Pattanaik, Devdutt. "HT Brunch Cover Story: 5 stories from the *Ramayana* you haven't heard before." *Hindustan Times*, 24 May 2020, https://www.hindustantimes.com/brunch/ht-brunch-cover-story-5-stories-from-the-*Ramayana*-you-haven-t-heard-before/story-nuCPzKqscCqJZTJAFJiF2K.html.

Rajhans, Gyan. "The Goddess Durga: The Mother of the Hindu Universe." *Learn Religions*, 14 January 2019, https://www.learnreligions.com/goddess-durga-1770363.

Sahota, Peter. "Creation in the Rig Veda. One of its several narratives in... | by Peter Sahota | Desire to Think." *Medium*, 23 February 2020, https://medium.com/desiretothink/creation-in-the-rig-veda-8772c3569d20.

Shreemaa. "Story of How Ravana Kidnapped Sita." *Devi Mandir*, 2023, https://www.shreemaa.org/story-how-ravana-kidnapped-sita/.

Singh, Soham. "The Hindu Mythology of India and Its Influence on Eastern Culture." *Gobookmart*, 3 January 2023, https://gobookmart.com/the-hindu-mythology-of-india-and-its-influence-on-eastern-culture/.

Sivananda, Sri Swami. "Ganesha – The Divine Life Society." *The Divine Life Society*, 2020, https://www.dlshq.org/religions/ganesha/.

TemplePurohit. "Ganesha Stories - 7 Most Popular Stories of Ganesha." *TemplePurohit*, 5 March 2022, https://www.templepurohit.com/ganesha-stories-7-popular-stories-of-ganesha/.

Trivedi, Raj. "Folktales from *Ramayana* – Talking Myths." *Talking Myths*, 2020, https://talkingmyths.com/category/folktale/folktales-from-*Ramayana*/.

University of British Columbia. "Vedic Theory of Creation." *UBC Computer Science*, 2006, https://www.cs.ubc.ca/~goyal/creation.php.

www.ingramcontent.com/pod-product-compliance
Lightning Source LLC
Chambersburg PA
CBHW070339010526
44107CB00004B/548